LOVEBIRDS AS A HOBBY

Kenny LeBreton

SAVE-OUR-PLANET SERIES

T.F.H. Publications, Inc.

1 T.F.H. Plaza • Third & Union Aves. • Neptune, NJ 07753

© Copyright 1992 by T.F.H. Publications, Inc.

Distributed in the UNITED STATES by T.F.H. Publications, Inc., One T.F.H. Plaza, Neptune City, NJ 07753; in CANADA to the Pet Trade by H & L Pet Supplies Inc., 27 Kingston Crescent, Kitchener, Ontario N2B 2T6; Rolf C. Hagen Ltd., 3225 Sartelon Street, Montreal 382 Quebec; in CANADA to the Book Trade by Macmillan of Canada (A Division of Canada Publishing Corporation), 164 Commander Boulevard, Agincourt, Ontario M1S 3C7; in ENGLAND by T.F.H. Publications, PO Box 15, Waterlooville PO7 6BQ; in AUSTRALIA AND THE SOUTH PACIFIC by T.F.H. (Australia) Pty. Ltd., Box 149, Brookvale 2100 N.S.W., Australia; in NEW ZEALAND by Ross Haines & Son, Ltd., 82 D Elizabeth Knox Place, Panmure, Auckland, New Zealand; in the PHILIPPINES by Bio-Research, 5 Lippay Street, San Lorenzo Village, Makati, Rizal; in SOUTH AFRICA by Multipet Pty. Ltd., P.O. Box 35347, Northway, 4065, South Africa. Published by T.F.H. Publications, Inc. Manufactured in the United States of America by T.F.H. Publications, Inc.

CONTENTS

Introduction

One of the most popular groups of birds that one can purchase today are those known as lovebirds. These birds are true parrots, and because of their small size they can be kept in accommodation both less expensive to purchase or build and which is quite small in comparison to that needed for many other parrots.

There are nine species of lovebirds, and all live in Africa or its

A peach-faced lovebird takes to the air. (R. & V. Moat)

nearby islands. Although they superficially resemble the parrotlets of South America they are not closely related to these birds and have become similar in appearance because both groups of birds have lifestyles and habitats which are not dissimilar.

The name *lovebird* stems from the fact that pair members are very

The cremino strain lovebird. (Michael Gilroy)

affectionate towards each other, but this affection is rarely extended to members of their own species—with whom they will often fight very savagely if in breeding condition. Even with other birds they are only safe with those who are somewhat larger than themselves, and this is because lovebirds are extremely tough little characters for their size and possess quite powerful beaks.

Only eight of the nine species are available to would-be owners, and of these eight only four are readily available to those living in Australia, the other four no longer being found on that continent due to import restrictions. Even in the UK and the USA only three of the eight species could be described as freely available, the others being rather scarce and expensive.

Lovebirds are ideal aviary birds, being relatively quiet, reliable breeders and, in the popular species, able to cope with most climates. Their diets are simple and pose no complications

The green pied (left) and blue pied lovebird strains are among the more attractive available to hobbyists. (Michael Gilroy)

that can be found in more exotic species and there is always a steady demand for any surplus stock. They are popular exhibition birds, and gaining more supporters in this area all of the time as a result of the numerous color mutations that are now available, especially in the peach-faced species.

As pet birds, lovebirds are inquisitive and very active birds, but it must be stressed that they do not have any talking ability worth considering, and they are not as easy to finger-tame unless they are

purchased when very young—preferably after having been hand-reared. Such birds make super pets if sufficient time is devoted to them—which is a fundamental essential with any of the parrot species, regardless of their size. They are reasonably long-lived for their size and ten years or even more would not be unusual.

In the following text the newcomer to these birds will find all of the information likely to be needed to successfully keep and breed them. No assumption of previous bird-keeping knowledge has been made, so the text covers lovebirds from every possible viewpoint, be this as aviary occupants, exhibition birds or as pets in the home.

This jade lovebird displays the bright-eyed, inquisitive nature characteristic of the group. (Michael Gilroy)

Accommodation

The housing needs of lovebirds can be divided into three basic types: outdoor aviaries, indoor to get underway with keeping the birds, this should not be done until suitable accommodation has been

Adequate aviary space is essential as lovebirds can be aggressive.

flights, and cages of various sizes. Although beginners are usually impatient prepared. Undoubtedly, aviaries are the finest ways in which to house your birds, indoor flights being a

Outdoor aviaries are suited only to warmer climates. (J.R. Quinn)

less expensive option, while cages are the least desirable accommodation—even for a pair of pet birds, unless these are to receive liberal free-flying time in your home. The comments in respect of aviaries must be qualified by adding that in the case of the less hardy species, such as the red-faced or Nyasas, outdoor aviaries are only possible as year 'round housing if you live in a year 'round warm climate; the northern states of the USA, as well as Canada, the UK and most of Europe would be too cold for these species during the winter. In these cases large indoor flights are best, but with access to an outdoor flight during the warmest months. In Australia these remarks also hold true in the colder months of the year, but of course apply specifically to the Nyasa, as the other three available species are much more hardy (Australia has only four of the eight species kept in captivity).

Aviaries

Before discussing essentials of aviaries it is worthwhile making one or two comments in respect of lovebirds as residents of these. Firstly, with the exception of the red-faced lovebird, which can be colony bred, all lovebirds should be kept in their own housing, per pair, if breeding is planned. I do not suggest that it is not possible to breed other species on a colony basis but simply that to do so is to take risks, as lovebirds are very aggressive birds when breeding and may well attack and injure other pairs in their flight. They will also attack the young of others sharing the same aviary. If attempts to keep more than one pair per flight are ever attempted, then it is vital such birds are housed in an extremely spacious aviary, a very costly undertaking. If lovebirds are to be housed in a mixed bird collection then they should be placed with species which are larger than they are, lovebirds being

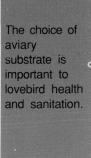

The choice of aviary substrate is important to lovebird health and sanitation.

The lovebird cage must be constructed of sturdy wire, not easily chewed wood! (David Alderton)

very tough for their size and often belying their name, which is a bit of a misnomer. Nor are these birds suitable for a planted aviary, as they will quickly destroy all but the strongest of branches and will strip the foliage bare.

Lovebirds will soon make short work of any vegetation in their aviary! (Glen S. Axelrod)

Aviary Site

You may have little choice in the site available, but if you do then choose a level site that is sheltered yet not directly under trees. Falling leaves become untidy and dampen the aviary, while overhead branches, beyond dropping rain on the flight, will also be used as perching sites for owls, cats and other animals whose presence will disturb the lovebirds, and wild birds perching overhead will also foul the aviary with their droppings. If your garden or yard has a slope to it, then do not place the aviary at the lowest point as this will also be the dampest spot. It is always better if the aviary is within the sight of your home so you are able to keep an eye on it.

Finally, choose a site that faces the south or east in order to benefit from the early morning sun and so as to avoid the northerly and westerly cold winds. If you live in Australia or elsewhere in the southern hemisphere then you need the site to face north or east for best protection and most sunshine.

Aviary Floor

The choice is bare earth, concrete, paving slabs, gravel or any mixture of these.

Bare Earth Other than the fact it is on site already, it has no other advantages, but many negatives. Firstly, it will soon become heavily fouled with the feces of both the lovebirds and those of wild birds; this represents a considerable health risk through soil contamination. It will quickly become a mud bath should you enter the aviary after rain has fallen, and it will also sprout numerous weeds. These may actually be appreciated by the birds but they will likely have been fouled with droppings and they tend to look untidy as well. Finally, unless you remove a top layer of earth and isolate the aviary base with netting of very small mesh, then it is probable that numerous unwanted visitors will burrow into the flight and cause considerable damage. If you have a large area available for your aviaries, then you

The sturdy nature of lovebird cage construction is evident in this photo.

could have small units that were fully welded wired on their base, and these could be moved around on a rotational basis. Such a system was very popular many years ago but is rarely seen these days.

Concrete This is easy to hose down and keep very clean. It should carry a slope to take away rainwater, and a channel to direct this out of the aviary. Such an outlet should be duly covered with a very small mesh to prevent the entry of unwanted visitors. Concrete is relatively easy to lay, especially useful if long lines of aviaries are to be permanently sited, but it is very final, this being its only real drawback. In order to improve its rather utilitarian look you could give it a covering of gravel, contained by a low perimeter wall to the whole site. An alternative, which is very effective, is to add a coloring agent to the concrete or to paint it with

Paving Slabs Personally, I find slabs to be my favorite at this time because they offer such flexibility of use. For one thing they can be lifted and relocated at another site. They come in a range of colors, sizes, and surface qualities from rough to very smooth. Placed onto a good bed of sand and gravel, the amount of weeds that will grow through the joints is negligible, and these are soon eaten by the lovebirds.

Gravel Coming in a range of sizes and natural colors, gravel is possibly the cheapest option other than bare earth, and certainly the quickest to put down. It can be raked over and hosed to keep droppings to a minimum, but

A beautiful pair of Fischer's lovebirds, *Agapornis fischeri.* (Harry V. Lacey)

one of the special concrete paints—say, a green. This will act as a sealant and will reduce the amount of concrete dust that would otherwise continually be found.

Aviary design can vary but should always allow for plenty of flying space. (J.R. Quinn)

still needs to be placed over a good strong mesh to prevent vermin from cntering the aviary. Lovebirds will enjoy pecking about in it for grit and invertebrates. In a large aviary a path of slabs is suggested, as gravel is not the easiest surface to walk on, dcpending on the depth to which it is laid.

Aviary Size

The dimensions of an aviary will be determined by various factors such as space available, number of birds to be housed, and, most important, available cash for the project. I would suggest that if a row of breeding aviaries is planned, then these should have a minimum width of 62cm (2ft), a length of 2m (6.5ft), and a height of minimum 2.1m (7ft). Obviously, if it is possible to increase these dimensions—especially the length—then this can only be to the good of the pairs, who will have more straight-line flying space in which to exercise. A point that should be given consideration when planning the size is the question of the widths of the welded wire that will be used in construction. Check out what sizes are available in your locality (though it can be purchased by mail-order from manufacturers or specialist sellers to the avicultural world who advertise in the national cage-bird magazines).

It is often better to have the aviary made of convenient panel widths which approximate the dimensions you want when they are bolted together.

Ready-made or Home-Built?

There are some superb ready-made

An attractive indoor cage, equipped with individual compartment trays for easy cleaning.(Scott Boldt)

aviaries available today, and these come in all shapes and qualities and simply need bolting together. You can pick and mix in many cases in order that the aviary is suited to your particular needs. However, the really cheap ones should be avoided as they will give you no service life at all because they will be made from less than substantial timbers and generally are not suited to the destructive beaks of lovebirds. It is suggested that you gather in the various catalogues from numerous producers of aviaries and ponder the merits very carefully. A visit to a few breeders of lovebirds has much to recommend it, as you will gain from their experiences; likewise, a visit to the larger bird shows should enable you to see and discuss the merits of on-site examples at the show. The handy person will probably prefer to build his own aviaries, as they can be done exactly to his specification and quality.

Aviary Frames

Although one could build a framework of wood onto which welded wire could be attached, it is usually easier, and more practical, to prepare a

Outdoor flights should be of sturdy construction and provide an overhang for protection from the elements. (David Alderton)

number of wooden frames of a manageable size and fix the welded wire onto these. Such frames can then be bolted together to the required aviary dimensions. This method will turn out somewhat more expensive but has the advantage that the whole structure can be dismantled and reassembled at another site. It can be added to without undue problems and repairs, when needed, are more easily and neatly effected. The timber for the frames should be a minimum of 5cm x 2.5cm (2 x 1in), which gives good strength. The frames should be treated with a suitable wood preservative before the wire is attached.

Metal Frames A rather more expensive aviary

frame would be one made from either angular or tubular metal, preferably of non-rusting quality. These will last a lifetime, and of course the lovebirds will not be able to whittle away at them as they can where wood is used. There are many light alloys on the market, and a visit to one or two engineering companies will give you a good idea of these. When you have calculated needed lengths, these companies will cut them to size and drill them to take fastening bolts. Those which fit into three-sided corner sleeves are better than having welded corners, as they can then be dismantled more easily. Metal corner pieces are available in a number of sizes to be used in conjunction with wood, and these are very useful. If wooden frames are used, then do ensure that the welded wire is stapled to the inner surfaces of the frames; otherwise, the wood will soon be the target of your lovebirds' beaks.

Welded Wire The most

This handsome cinnamon lutino sports an identification band, a good idea if you keep many birds. (Michael Gilroy)

usual gauge that is found on lovebird aviaries will be 19G, though 16G is better but more expensive. Likewise, 2.5 x 1.25cm (1 x 0.5in) mesh size is the most popular but, again,this is because it is cheaper than 1.25 x 1.25cm, which is actually more suitable in that it will restrict even small mice from entering, which the slightly large hole size will not. Any hole size larger than the two quoted will not only allow mice to enter but may also be large enough for weasels to get through, and these mustelids can cause havoc in no time at all. Breeders in Europe are largely free from the risk of snakes but in Australia and the USA there are numerous members of the family Colubridae that can get through quite small mesh and will attempt to devour any birds

they can get at, especially chicks in the nest. Butcher birds are probably the biggest nuisance to Australian breeders, so meshing either sides of the frames may be required to give protection to the lovebirds. Double meshing is advised between adjoining aviaries, as this will elimi- nate the risk of birds having their feet or beaks damaged as a result of fighting between pairs in adjacent aviaries.

In order to both prolong the welded wire's life and to

Colubrid snakes, rodents, and mustelids (weasels) can create problems for the aviculturist. (Michael Gilroy and R.D. Bartlett)

improve your view of the lovebirds, a coat of black bituminous paint should be applied to the wire. Allow this to thoroughly dry before allowing birds into the aviary.

that you can service the aviaries efficiently. In the warmer climates an enclosed shelter is not the essential which it is in Europe, the northerly states of the USA, and similar places that can have quite dramatic seasonal fluctuations in temperatures. In the open-type aviaries the lovebirds will roost in their nest boxes if they feel cold, and these boxes should be hung in a sheltered part of the aviary.

This compact show cage is not suited as permanent lovebird quarters! (H. R. Axelrod)

Aviary Design

The most common shape for an aviary is a rectangular box style, but octagonal aviaries are gaining in popularity and are very attractive. There is really no limit to possibilities— the main essential being

Safety Porches

In a row of aviaries it is worth having a safety passage running the length of the aviaries. Upon entering this corridor and securely closing the door behind you, you can then enter the individual aviaries without fear that a bird might fly past you and away. A useful idea is to have a door at the opposite end of the passage leading into a larger aviary that can be used to stock young birds after they have fledged. In this manner these birds can be allowed out of their flights, into the passage, and thus then be ushered down into the stock aviary; they need not be caught up, and this saves them being frightened by this process.

Wind and Rain Protection

It is worth-while attaching plastic panels to the outside of the aviaries during inclement weather—only one third of the aviary needs to be clad along the sides and roof, over the feeding and nesting area. During the summer, tinted panels can be placed over part of the roof, and these will provide shade from the sun. Alternatively, wattling looks nice and allows diffused sunshine to filter through. The lovebirds must always be able to escape the direct rays of the sunshine, which otherwise could cause them much discomfort. In such breeding aviaries the nest boxes can be so fixed

A splendid lutino strikes an engaging pose. (Michael Gilroy)

This wooden nest box is equipped with a metal collar to prevent chewing by the lovebirds.

A bright-eyed pair of normal-type peach-faced lovebirds. (H.R. Axelrod)

that they can be inspected without the need to enter the aviary; likewise, either a hanging feeding station, or one on a shelf, should be so positioned that it can be serviced from the outside via a small service hatch.

Aviary Furnishings

The internal fittings of the aviary will be a single perch at the opposite end of the flight from the nest boxes, and a good-sized but very shallow drinking and bathing earthenware dish on the aviary floor. A perch will be required near the feeding station and to give access to nesting boxes. This is all that is needed in a small aviary,

which should not be cluttered so that it impedes

straight-flying space. Obviously, in a larger aviary one has more scope to use imagination to both the benefit of the birds and to create esthetic appeal for yourself. Extra branches of various thickness will be welcome, and you could place a large pecking tray on the floor (but not under branches where it could be fouled with feces). In such a tray you could place earth or a turf of grass which will be appreciated by the lovebirds; it is easily replaced once they have had a good rummage in it. In a really large display aviary, a rocklike wall which has numerous small ledges on it will be well used by the birds. The object in such aviaries is to provide the birds with as many interesting objects as you can, so that they have plenty to amuse themselves with, which is important to their mental state.

Indoor Flights

Indoor flights should be as spacious as is possible and may well be as large as a small outdoor aviary— or sometimes even larger, depending on the available building they are in and how many birds you comfortably feel you can devote sufficient time to. Lovebirds will happily breed in such accommodation, which should be as light and airy as possible. All windows in such a building should be covered with welded wire to prevent birds escaping should they get out of their flights while an exterior window is open; also, this saves them dashing against the glass with potentially fatal results. The floor of indoor flights should be such that

A variety of perch fastenings; make sure all materials are sturdy!

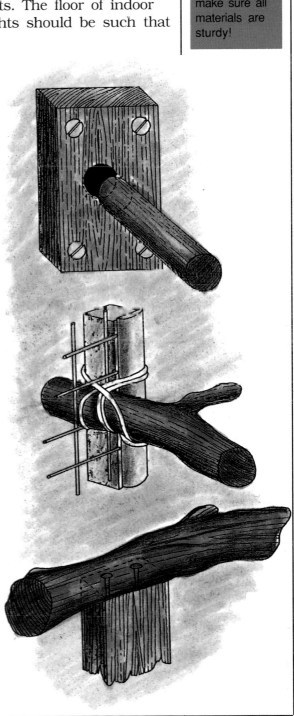

it can easily be washed, and there are numerous brands of excellent stiff linoleum tiles that can be used with this in mind. Walls should be smooth and painted a bright cheerful color; one of the pastel shades of green would be very effective. The building

wise, come the spring when the birds are allowed into outdoor flights, they are at greater risk of a chill. In any case, prior to warmer weather, indoor aviaries should be equalized in temperature with that of the outside.

Peach-faced, Abyssinian, Fischer's and masked

Cutaway drawing of a lovebird "intensive care" unit, or hospital cage, showing controlled heat source.

lovebirds are the hardiest of the genus, so any heating in their flights will be as much for your own working comfort as for any need on their behalf. Tubular or the latest fan-type heaters are the most reliable and safest form of heating. They are better, and more economical, for being wired through a thermostat to ensure a steady, non-fluctuating temperature. Sudden

containing the flights should be draftproof but it is not essential that it is heated—except during especially cold periods and then only sufficiently to take the chill from the air. If nest boxes are not installed in the flights, then the temperature can be raiséd slightly so the birds are not cold. But do not go overboard with heat, other-

changes in temperature will rapidly result in your stock suffering with health problems. If the birds have bred during the summer,

then it is not recommended to encourage overwinter breeding as most certainly the vigor of the young produced will not be as good as natural summer clutches. This so, nest boxes should be removed and possibly the pair split up—though established pairs will be more subject to stress if this is done, so treat each pair on their merits—a fact that should be applied to all aspects of their care.

Useful Extras

Because the air in an enclosed bird room is more subject to bacterial build-up than is an outside

flight, I would recommend the purchase of one or more ionizers. These release millions of negative ions into the air around them, and these engulf debris and bacteria which they render more easily wiped from the unit itself and from the floor where the ions settle. They range in price based on their performance, and they can be plugged into a normal light socket; running costs are minimal, but remember that you may need two or more depending on the size of the room they are to operate in.

Lighting There is a considerable range of lighting that can be used to good effect in an indoor situation. One of

Two approaches to outdoor aviary construction; note the damage done by the birds' chewing activity. (Glen S. Axelrod)

the more recent developments has been the availability of black light (it is actually dark blue). These tubes release light in the ultraviolet range and are so

very useful overwinter when little sunshine is available. There are numerous brands of fluorescent strips that produce light similar to that of daylight, and it is worthwhile contacting a specialist lighting company to see which lighting they stock. Avoid the normal-type ultraviolet daylight bulbs now available because these also generate much heat, which is not desirable for birds.

Night Lights It is recommended that you install a night light in your bird room, and this can either be a very low wattage white light but is better for being a soft color—blue being a good choice. If you feed your lighting through a dimmer and timer, then as the main lights go out, the night lights can come on. This saves plunging the birds into sudden darkness, while the night light will ensure that any birds startled from their roosting perch will be able to find their way back, rather than sitting on the floor or clinging for maybe hours to the flight netting.

Avicultural Magazines In order to keep abreast of all the latest developments—and where they can be obtained—I would recommend all lovebird breeders and owners to subscribe to their national cage-bird magazines. For a modest price you get an awful lot of up-to-date news, views and ads of products.

Oftentimes, pet shops carry a variety of pet periodicals for hobbyists.

Cages

Although most pet lovebirds are housed in all-wire

cages, these are not actually the most desirable. Lovebirds are somewhat nervous creatures, and so prefer housing which affords some sense of security. With this in mind the box-type cages with wired fronts are better. This type is used by breeders and comes as single, double or treble breeder— with removable sliding partitions that enable the flight length to increase as each divider is removed. A good size for a pair of lovebirds would be 93cm long by 38cm deep by 62cm high (3ft x 15in x 2ft).

Should you purchase the all-wire type then site it near to a wall, maybe in a corner, where the birds will have security on two sides. An even better arrangement for housing pet birds would be to build an indoor flight cage into an alcove. This would give them much more space to fly about in and can be made to look extremely attractive by using paneled woods which are grained to various natural patterns from oak to rosewood. Cages require pull-out trays to facilitate easy cleaning, though some all-wire models are built onto plastic bases which simply unclip so that the top lifts off. Beware if such cages have any exposed plastic

edges, as a lovebird will make short shrift of these! Perches are normally of doweling, and today there are also plastic perches produced but though easy to clean I do not favor these at all as they are wholly unnatural. In fact, even one of the doweling perches in a cage is better

Smaller cages are quite suitable for single birds, such as budgerigars, but lovebirds should not be kept alone.

removed and replaced with a natural branch of variable thickness—this is much better for the birds' feet, which will be exercised on such. Doweling can be

this is good therapy for a pet bird's beak. A final point about cages for lovebirds is that the metal bars of these are better if they run across the cage rather than vertically; lovebirds enjoy clambering up and down the bars. Have a good look

A finger-tamed lovebird makes a far superior pet! (Risa Teitler)

roughed up with sand paper or notches cut into it with a sharp knife. Small notches help the bird get a better grip, which is most important where breeding stock is concerned. Natural perches will be whittled away by the lovebirds but are easily replaced, and

around before purchasing a cage, because you will probably only purchase one; get the best and largest possible from the outset—avoid tall narrow cages, as these are of no use to the birds. Select one with good length, the longer the better, and one which is a simple box shape so the bird can use all the available space.

Feeding

Lovebirds are extremely easy birds to feed, requiring no especially hard-to-come-by food in order to maintain peak health and good breeding condition. However, this is not to suggest that their menu should be chosen without due consideration of the fact that the diet must be well balanced and

ing the actual foods lovebirds prefer, let us consider feeding utensils and other general aspects of nutritional husbandry.

Feeding Utensils

It makes no difference to your lovebirds what sort of containers their food and water is in as long as it is

contain those items which are essential for good body metabolism. The key to success lies in providing a good variety of food items, for in this way the chances of a needed vitamin or mineral being deficient will be greatly reduced; at the same time you are thus less likely to be feeding an excess of a given item. Before discuss-

supplied. It is thus a matter of convenience and personal opinion which containers are preferred.

Seed This can be supplied in open dishes which are freestanding or hung on the

This peach-faced lovebird is enjoying a snack from a well-stocked food tray. (Dr. H.R. Axelrod)

A peach-faced lovebird chomps on an unripe cherry. (Michael Gilroy)

cage or aviary sides, or it can be supplied in gravity-fed automatic feeders of numerous styles. Open dishes are best made of earthenware as these are heavy so not easily thrown about by the lovebirds, and are easily cleaned. Plastic dishes will soon be tipped over unless they are the D-shaped kind which are hooked onto the cage wires. Open dishes may become fouled with feces and will need the husks blown from them each day—otherwise the pots may appear to contain seed when actually they only contain husks.

On the credit side, the fact that they must be checked daily does ensure you spend at least some time in monitoring the individual habits of your lovebirds and so will more readily notice if a bird or a pair have consumed their usual rations. If not, this might be the early-warning indicator that they are not well. Automatic feeders have improved over the years and are not quite as

prone to clogging as were those of years ago—even so, they can still get clogged, so it pays to tap each feeder to ensure the seed is being dispensed without problem. Models vary from simple tubes with plastic bases through to large chicken-style metal containers for those with numerous birds in a flight. The best of these have adjustable openings which can thus be made to suit the size of the seed.

You can also purchase jam-jar feeders, which are plastic or wooden bases onto which a jam or preserves jar is placed in an inverted position.

Water Again, open dishes can be used, but these days most breeders use the self-dispenser type, as the water stays fresher and is much less liable to become fouled with feces, debris or seed; even so they should be refilled each day so the water is always fresh. The green algae that forms on the inside will not harm your birds—but any bacteria on it might do so; thus it should be cleaned off every week.

Other Containers Captive bred birds lead a rather lazy life compared to their wild brethren, so it is useful to try and make them work a little for certain food items—this is good for their mental as well as their physical well-being. One way this can be done is to place favored goodies into hanging containers made of wire mesh of differing sizes. These can be hung in the flight so that the birds need to hang on at differing angles while trying to nibble the food. You can no doubt devise numerous ways which will require a certain degree of dexterity on the

Choose lovebird foods with care; they should have both visual appeal and nutritional value. (David Alderton)

Three of the many feeder designs on the market today. Most have adjustable openings to suit the type of seeds offered.

love-bird's behalf in order to gain the tidbit.

Winnowers These machines separate husks from uneaten seed, and manufacturers claim up to 95% of seed placed through them is saved. They range in price according to construction and are a worthwhile consideration.

Mixed or Single Seeds?

Some owners feed their birds with a seed mixture while others prefer to feed each seed variety in separate pots. If you only have a pair of pet lovebirds, then it is probably more convenient to purchase a mixed packet of seed and supply this in a single pot, for the amount wasted will not amount to a great deal of money. However, where a number of

pairs are kept, then clearly economy is worthwhile. If a seed mixture is given, then the birds will first of all eat their preferred seed—often throwing other seeds out of the dish in the process. On a large scale this adds up to a sizable lump of cash, so it is better to feed each seed type in its own container.

Feeding Routine

The time of day when you feed your birds is not critical—though by nature most birds are actively feeding during the early and late periods of the day, resting during the hotter parts. What is important is that you choose a regular time and stick with it as far as possible, as birds are creatures of routine (as are all animals, including us humans). Always ensure you spend a few moments watching each bird feeding so that you are sure all is well. In large collections it is so easy to overlook this aspect, yet when you reach that point where you do not seem to have the time to monitor individual birds, then that should tell you that either help is needed or you should thin down your stock to a more manageable size. Quality of husbandry is always far better, and cheaper, than quantity of stock.

Types of Food

In broad terms, all food will provide one or more of three basic essentials; it will also provide, in varying amounts, three other needed components of health. We will divide these into bulk foods and non-bulk foods.

Bulk Foods

Carbohydrates

These compounds are needed to produce energy for day-to-day muscular activity. During the course of activity a byproduct is, of course, heat. Cereal crops are the main source of carbohydrates and for lovebirds the seeds most favored are normally a mixture of canary seed and one or more of the millets; the ratio is 50:50, but this is not essential, though a useful guide. Again, it is not important which country these seeds come from, though in reality you will find that the price will reflect this fact, some, such as Moroccan and Spanish canary seed being more expensive, and generally of better quality, than that of Australia, Canada, the USA and elsewhere. Likewise, Japanese millet is invariably higher priced than that from Italy and elsewhere. White millet is preferred to yellow millet. Wheat, maize and oats or groats are other forms of

Self-dispensing type water units are superior to open dishes; dispensers should be cleaned often in warm weather.

A wide variety of seeds is available at well-stocked pet shops.

cereals which are rich in carbohydrates, though less frequently given to lovebirds.

Proteins and Fats These provide the other two needed bulk foods. Proteins are required in order to build or replace body tissues, while fats are required both to provide body insulation and to assist in other metabolic processes. Both proteins and fats can be stored in the body to create a reserve source of energy and are quickly converted into starches—carbohydrates. Should this happen on an excessive scale then it produces the condition known as going light—in which the muscle tissue of the chest is lacking such that the breast bone becomes visible and the muscle on the thighs likewise is greatly reduced. Numerous

A fine example of the normal cinnamon peach-faced lovebird. (Michael Gilroy)

seeds are rich in proteins and fats, the two being found together in seeds. The one most commonly fed to lovebirds is striped sunflower; there is also a white and a black variety of this seed but these are not greatly liked by lovebirds, especially not the black. Choose the small seeds, which will normally be found to contain as much seed as do the larger hulled varieties, thus in these latter varieties you are paying more for the hull than for the seed. Other protein-and fat-rich seeds are hemp, niger, maw and rape, but these are not especially popular with lovebirds, hemp being the most likely to be taken. In recent years both pea-nuts and pine nuts have found great favor with parrot owners. Both are rich in proteins and fats, the latter somewhat more so than the former—do not feed salted peanuts to your birds, and choose those graded as fit for human consumption. Of course, any seeds can be offered to your lovebirds, who will also be found to enjoy the seeding heads of grasses, many berries, and seeds such as sesame and lin-seed. All seeds must be clean and free of any signs of contamination by ro-dents—as well as being

free of dust and any other debris. Always be prepared to pay the going rate for quality—there is no such thing as cheap, quality seed in this day and age. A very popular seed with most birds, including lovebirds, is millet in the

ear—known as millet sprays. These can be hung up in a convenient position and will be greatly enjoyed; they can also be given after being soaked in water.

Soaked Seed

It will be found that by soaking seeds for 24 hours

Mixed fruit and seed foods may be on the expensive side but are well worth the extra cost.

The covered hut-type feeder is a good choice for large, open aviaries containing many birds.

these will be relished by most lovebirds, and it is a useful way of tempting your birds to try a seed they hitherto had never been given. Simply place the seeds in water overnight or for 24 hours and then thoroughly rinse them in a sieve before feeding. Soaked seeds can be

A young jade lovebird. (Michael Gilroy)

germinated by placing them on a tray, after soaking, and putting them in a darkened cupboard with a controlled temperature for 24–48 hours. Once they are sprouting small shoots, they can be washed and fed to your lovebirds, who will relish them in this form. During germination the protein level increases, as does the vitamin level, so these seeds will be appreciated by hens with chicks to rear, as well as by birds which are recovering from an illness.

Obesity

One problem to watch out for when feeding protein-rich seeds to your birds is overweight. In the non-breeding season, keep protein seeds to a minimum, increasing them prior to breeding and maybe during cold-weather spells, when they will be appreciated.

Non-Bulk Foods

Under this heading comes vitamins, minerals and non-plant proteins, as well as any supplements that you decide to give your birds.

Vitamins The richest source of vitamins will be greenfoods, root crops and fruits. Such foods are of course bulk foods, but the bulk is composed of water in such foods—as much as 95% in lettuce, while even in apples it is 83% and in carrots 87%. The list of potential foods under this heading is so vast that only typical examples need be given. Cabbage, spinach, cress, celery and Brussels sprouts are obvious culti-vated greenfoods, while dandelion, shepherd's purse, chickweed and clover are useful wild plants—care should be taken to always wash these in case they have been sprayed with harmful chemicals or fouled by dogs or motor fumes. Root crops include carrots, beet and turnips, while fruit will range from apples to or-anges, grapes to pomegran-ates. Do not forget figs, which are important to some species, and you are always safe to offer any

Fresh fruits and vegetables supply captive lovebirds with roughage in addition to essential vitamins and minerals.

An adult pair of Fischer's lovebirds. (Harry V. Lacey)

berries that are eaten by wild birds: rose-hips, blackberries and the like. Small twigs, including the leaves, of fruit trees and non-poisonous trees will be greatly appreciated by your birds, as these will provide both amusement and useful roughage. They can be hung in the aviary

or simply clamped together where the lovebirds will enjoy climbing among them until they have destroyed them. Do not suddenly overfeed any greenfoods—especially of fresh wild plants in the spring—as this will prompt diarrhea. Supply a steady amount throughout the year, and the bird should encounter no problems as it will not be tempted to overfeed on them as it would if they are offered only sporadically.

Minerals The important minerals required in relatively large amounts are calcium and phosphorus, and these are supplied via cuttlefish bone or by calcium powder. Oyster shell and crushed eggshells are other sources of these elements. Other minerals are required in smaller quantities and are termed *trace elements*. They include iodine, magnesium, zinc, copper and cobalt. Provided you are feeding

a varied diet, then the need for trace elements will be met within this, and so should never be a cause for concern. However, calcium intake rises dramatically in a hen when she is producing eggs, so this should be available throughout the year.

Non-Plant Proteins Proteins are composed of

This lovebird shows signs of good care: bright eyes, clean, sharp bill, and good feathering. (Vince Serbin)

amino acids, and all of these that are needed by birds are not available purely from plant sources, so a certain quantity of animal proteins should be provided in order to ensure a complete diet. Examples of animal proteins are invertebrates, such as earthworms, maggots and other insect larvae as well as insects themselves; and cheese, milk, meat extracts, and of course meat itself. Bread soaked in milk is often given to hens with young to rear, and is use-

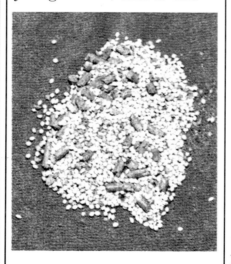

fully fed to stock as an occasional treat throughout the year. Lovebirds differ greatly in their willingness to take animal proteins, so only trial and error will establish which are preferred. Beyond feeding these in their normal state you can produce all manner of mashes, or you can pur-

chase canary-rearing foods or insectivore food already packaged at your local pet store. Again, these are useful during the breeding season when chicks need high-protein diets to give them a good start in life. In the wild, few birds feed on the same diet throughout the year; it varies both as different plants flower or fruit, and when the birds are breeding, for they will start to take various insects and no doubt a certain amount of carrion.

Grit

All birds need to consume an amount of grit in order to aid in the digestion of seed. With no teeth to macerate seed into pulp, this is effected by the action of the bird's stomach muscles together with the grit. Once the latter has lost its sharp edges it is expelled in the feces. The size of the grit is important, so you should tell your dealer that it is for lovebirds. Birds having access to flights will pick over the floor area if this contains gravel, but even so mineralized grit should always be available in a pot and maybe also scattered on the floor—which is where lovebirds in the wild would collect it.

Grit is an important aid to digestion in lovebirds and should be offered in plentiful supply. (Isabelle Francais)

Water

All birds have a negative water position in respect of their bodily needs. If your birds receive a good supply of fruits and greenfood then their need to drink water will reduce—but it will still be there. Water is also gained from seeds during body metabolism but, overall, intake from all food sources is still always lower than the loss from respiration and that expelled via feces, so ensure the birds always have available to them a clean, fresh water supply. If they have been provided with any sort of bathing facilities then they will invariably choose this to drink from instead of their regular supply, which should still be maintained.

Feeding Habits

It is often said that animals instinctively know which foods are good for them and which are not; however, this is unlikely to be totally true. In reality, your lovebirds' feeding habits are more acquired than instinctive. A chick is given food by its parents, and this sets the pattern of what it will accept later in life; this pattern may be modified if the chick sees other birds eating a given food it has not itself tried—seeing them eat it will prompt the chick to try it, just as your children's habits will directly reflect what you gave them as babies and what you eat yourself. If you are confronted with something you have never tried before, then your instinct is to leave it alone. But if someone else tells you it is superb, then you may overcome your distrust of the unknown and give it a try.

This will either confirm your initial thoughts of not liking it, or you will be pleasantly surprised, after which it will be incorporated in your diet. Your birds are exactly the same, and if given a spartan diet by their breeder they will be very reluctant to even sample other foods, unless they see other lovebirds enjoying such foods! Again, feeding habits and tastes do change with age, so that an item disliked as a youngster may be relished

Nearly all cagebirds appreciate a bath now and then and the lovebird is no exception! (J.R. Quinn)

as that youngster grows into an adult—and vice versa. It is important, therefore, that we should not give up on our birds just because a food is initially refused. Later in the year it may be accepted, or maybe if we remove a popular item for a few hours the new one will be sampled. The greater variety of foods your birds will take, then the greater variety will their youngsters accept, thus making them easier birds to feed, and a pattern of progress is thus in hand.

For centuries the feeding of birds—and many other aspects of their husbandry—made virtually no progress at all because one generation after the other

Your pet shop or bird store can advise you on the kinds of vitamins and food supplements available and their recommended use. (Isabelle Francais)

lived on handed-down dogmas about what should and should not be done. Only when breeders started to experiment did aviculture really start to make big strides forward.

By studying the flora and fauna of the birds' natural habitat, one may be prompted to try this or that food on the birds. Do not let other people put you off just because their birds refuse a given item—maybe they are not as talented or patient as you are in persuading the birds to try it.

When you purchase your initial stock it is best to stick with the diet supplied by the pet shop or breeder. If it is a good diet, then stay with it; but if you feel it could be improved, then

introduce the additional items one at a time and in moderation.

Food Supplements

Given a good, wholesome and varied diet, your stock will require no extra sup-

extra supplements whatsoever. The use of multivitamin powders and liquids is very popular today—to the point that some breed-

ers are convinced that without such their breeding results would dramatically drop. This may be so, but this would merely underline the fact that such pep products were temporarily masking an obvious deficiency in their stock, because no bird in a healthy, fit, vigorous state should need to be dependent on concentrated vitamin and mineral tonics. If you have reason to believe your birds are suffering from any form of nutritional deficiency then you should discuss this with your veterinarian—not the man next door who knows everything about feeding birds! Your vet will advise what supplements should be given—or he may pinpoint the problem which may have nothing to do with feeding; it may stem from the breeding, the housing, the lack of exercise or an ailment.

A veterinarian skilled in the treatment of bird diseases may be difficult to find, so preventive care is the watchword! (Louise Van der Meid)

Practical Breeding

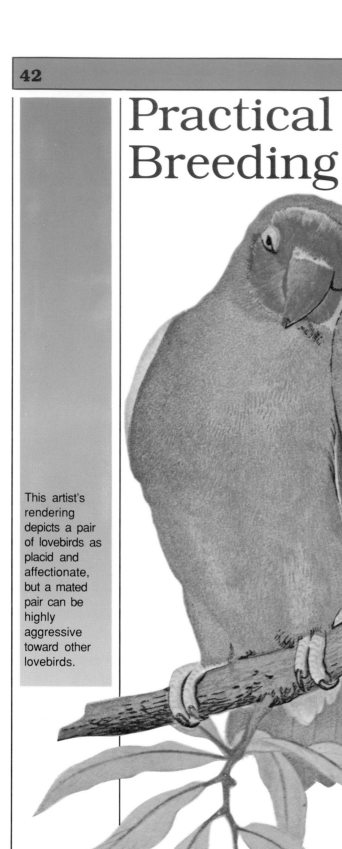

This artist's rendering depicts a pair of lovebirds as placid and affectionate, but a mated pair can be highly aggressive toward other lovebirds.

The three popular love-birds—peach-faced, masked and Fischer's—are all reliable and ready breeders, the other species somewhat less so, with Swindern's (the black-collared) being an unknown quantity as this species is not available in aviculture. The most difficult species to establish is the red-faced, and this is because their breeding habits are different from the others and they require very special nest boxes. They are also not at all suited to colder parts of the world; however, they have been bred in the UK and Europe—especially in Portugal—as well as in the USA and elsewhere.

Sexing

The first major problem a breeder has is to acquire a true pair, and this is because each of the popular species is sexually similar. Those species in which the sexes are physically different are referred to as being dimorphic (two forms). In lovebirds these are the Abyssinian, the red-faced and the Ma-

dagascar. It is possible to surgically sex birds, and this is now quite common in larger parrots but not in lovebirds. It is also possible to microscopically analyze the feces for indications of sex hormones, while analysis for sex chromosomes is yet another method for establishing the sex of a bird. However, these methods are not as yet very widespread, so there are no

A pair of masked lovebirds. This species breeds readily in captivity. (H. Reinhard)

sure ways of establishing the sex of your birds other than in the following two, somewhat obvious, ways: (1) If a lovebird lays an egg, then clearly it is a female. (2) If that egg is fertile then the other bird is a cock. There are other methods used by breeders, such as the pelvic-bone test, where the distance between these (wider in the hen) may be a guide. However, immatures and non breeding hens will feel the

same as cocks, so it is not a reliable method. Likewise, the size of the birds, the shape of their heads and

A pastel blue lovebird. (Michael Gilroy)

their general habits are also used as guides, but in each case there is no guarantee these observations will prove correct; of these, habits are possibly the best indicator. For example, if one bird is seen to continually try to mate with another then this is probably a cock—and likewise if two lovebirds frequent their nest box on a regular basis then they are probably hens—but the word *probably* still has to be emphasized. If eggs are laid, you then have to establish which of the two birds laid them, so it can be seen that lovebirds do not make things easy for breeders! A final method used is to release a number of lovebirds into an aviary containing plenty of nest boxes. The sexes will usually form true pairs—after some squabbling and fighting—but the system has been used successfully. Once pairs are formed, then the remaining unpaired birds must be removed if you decide to let the birds breed on a colony basis, which is not normally recommended in other than an extremely spacious aviary. Red-faced and Fischer's lovebirds are both colony breeders in the wild, so these will be found to be the more reliable on this system. Given these difficulties, it is obviously worthwhile paying out a higher price to purchase proven pairs, as this can save you much time. It is also a strong case for fitting closed bands to chicks because if these are numbered then once the

sex of the bird has been established you will have a record of this, thereby eliminating the chance of your being unsure should the bird be released into

A lutino peach-faced lovebird, one of the more popular varieties with hobbyists. (Michael Gilroy)

an aviary containing others of the same species.

Breeding Condition and Season

Once a pair has been acquired then they should not be bred from unless both are really in fit condition. The temptation to use them even though one is slightly out of condition should be resisted—no matter how keen you are to get underway. It will result in less-than-vigorous chicks, increasing the risk of egg binding if it is the hen, and could result in the death of the hen—so it just is not worth the risk. Pairs should have had good

The sky's the limit where it comes to lovebird nest boxes—as long as the design is sturdy and easily cleaned between use by breeders.

aviary time in which to exercise. Aviary-bred birds are always preferred to cage-bred birds, as they are hardier and more

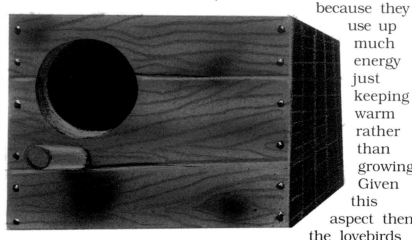

reliable breeders—a point to check out when buying your breeding stock. The normal breeding season for lovebirds is from the spring through summer. However, because lovebirds roost in their nest boxes, which must therefore in be in position the year 'round, they will continue to breed over winter if allowed to, and may rear clutches during

this period. Such clutches are much more at risk of death by freezing or chilling, apart from which they are generally more weak because they use up much energy just keeping warm rather than growing. Given this aspect then, the lovebirds should be taken indoors during the winter in colder regions and the nest boxes removed. Even this does not prevent prolific pairs from attempting to lay eggs and rear them, so separation may be the last resort, placing them in adjoining cages so they can still see and touch each other.

Nest Boxes

The usual nest box supplied to lovebirds (other than for the red-faced) is a rectangular box with dimensions of approximately 18cm wide x 20cm deep x 25.5cm high (7 x 8 x 10in) external measurements. It should be robustly constructed, using wood at least 1.25cm (0.5in) thick but is better for being .5cm (1in)—especially at its base, as it is not unknown for lovebirds to whittle away at this until they actually gnaw through the floor. The risk of this happening can be eliminated by covering the base—and extending just onto the sides—with a metal gauze

or aluminum. The roof of the nest box should include a hinged lid so that inspection of the box is possible without the risk of the chicks tumbling out of the nest box, which may happen if side doors are fitted. If the nest box is to be sited in the open part of the aviary, then the roof should slightly slope to the rear, and have an overhang all around it to take away rainwater—and a piece of roofing felt will render it more waterproof. However, it is better if it is sited under the covered part of the aviary. It should be placed well up in the aviary, around head height or somewhat higher, and such that, ideally, it can be inspected from the outside, thus not disturbing the adults. Inspection should be done while the pair are away feeding, if possible, especially with species which otherwise might desert the nest. It is always better to install two nest boxes per pair because this gives them a choice; in the case of colony-bred birds, then ensure the boxes are all in similar sites otherwise squabbling will ensue

for the more favored positions.

Entrance Hole Although many breeders place the entrance hole central to the front of the nest box, it is probably better placed well to one side—and high up—as this restricts the entry of sunlight, which the birds prefer. Likewise, do not make the hole too

Lovebird clutches vary between one and eight, with three to five being the average. (S. Bischoff)

large as is sometimes done; in fact, a tight fit is better as this will give the lovebirds something to work at, which will also help bring them into peak breeding condition. Just below the entrance hole a landing perch should be fitted.

Internal Ladder If you decide to use a nest box much taller than normal, then attach small strips of wood, ladder fashion, on the inside below the entrance hole. This facilitates easier exit by adults, and later the chicks. Do not use wire mesh, as is

sometimes advocated, because it has not been unknown for a chick or adult to get themselves caught up in this by their claws. It is useful if you construct the nest box using screws rather than nails; in this way it can be periodically dismantled in order to be subjected to

very thorough cleaning, and a light going-over with a blow torch to kill off any bacteria, mites or molds that may have established

themselves in the crevices. Often it is better just to discard the boxes once the lovebirds have used them for two or three seasons, depending on how much damage they have inflicted on them.

Nesting Material

The genus *Agapornis* is very unusual, though not quite unique, among parrots in that its members build nests, as opposed to laying their eggs on the bare base of the nest chamber. Materials are transported either tucked under the wings or amongst the feathers of the back. Dried grasses, twigs, leaves and similar material is added to the wood that has been chewed away inside the nest box. Provision of suitable material is thus essential during breeding operations, and a lining of peat gives them a useful start. What has been successfully tried is to fill the inside of the nest box with a cube of cork. It must be tight fitting. The lovebirds then whittle away to create a nest exactly to their preferred size—which is often rather smaller than that provided by

ourselves, as they like the sense of security a smaller nest provides.

Humidity

The relative humidity within the nest box is believed to have considerable effect upon the viability of eggs—and given the tropical conditions under which most species live, it is usually a case that this is too low in most countries

Lovebird chicks in nest box. Note the evidence of feather picking on the birds' backs. (Louise Van der Meid)

outside of Africa. During hot periods it will be worthwhile to lightly spray the outside of the nest box and to ensure the adults have good bathing facilities, both of which will increase humidity in the nest. The adults will return with damp plumage after bath-

sirable, as the eggs will be unable to lose water by evaporation and the chicks may drown in their shells. Humidity is still far from being well understood in aviculture, but our knowledge of it will steadily increase as more breeders study this aspect and

Lovebird eggs and fledglings. The hen usually begins to incubate after the second egg has been laid. (Louise Van der Meid)

ing. A supply of bark standing in water will also aid matters, as this will be used by the birds as nesting material. If you are breeding indoors, then besides spraying the nest boxes, it is suggested that you place a couple of pails of water in the breeding room—duly covered with mesh—as this will increase humidity on warm days. Excess humidity is not de-

record their findings—a hygrometer is therefore useful for you to record relative humidities.

Laying and Incubation

The clutch size in lovebirds can vary from 1–8 eggs, with 3–5 being the average. The eggs are incubated in 21–24 days, depending on when the hen commenced sitting in earnest—usual after the second egg. Fledging occurs after 38–45 days, and during this time the cock

will be involved more and more with the feeding of the growing youngsters. If the weather is somewhat cold for the time of year (usually the case in the UK!), then incubation may take an extra day or two. The hen does virtually all of the incubating, as the cock only enters the nest overnight to sleep with his partner. A quick glance into the nest box while the adults are away is all that should be done at this time, and this purely to check if eggs have been laid. Once the probable full clutch has been laid, then you can start counting off days, and by seven days after the last egg should have hatched you can check to see the result. If no eggs have hatched, then the mating was ineffectual and the eggs can be re-moved; the hen will likely re-mate and lay a second round. If the pair were wintered indoors, then clear eggs may result in the first round but things are usually fine after this.

Egg Binding

A distressing and potentially fatal problem is caused when a hen cannot release an egg from her vent. If you see the hen straining at all or lying in obvious discomfort on the aviary or cage floor, then she must be immediately placed in a warmed

hospital cage. This should effect release of the problem egg—if not call your vet immediately, as the egg must be removed surgically or the hen will die. This condition may be due to lack of calcium, overweight, or lack of overall condition—poorly conditioned muscles can't push the egg along

Lovebird eggs and fledgling. The incubation period for lovebirds is between 21 and 24 days.

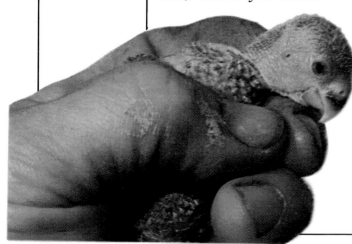

Very young lovebirds in the downy stage (upper) and at one week of age (lower). (Mervin F. Roberts)

the oviduct). Once the hen has recovered, she should not be used again that season for breeding. Any eggs already laid should be placed under other love-birds with eggs, or you may attempt to place them in an incubator and then hand-rear them, which is possible but extremely difficult from such an early age. A sudden cold spell might also make a hen egg bound; therefore, if the weather is at a changeable time, I would be tempted to take the birds indoors as they will have a better chance of rearing late-in-the-year chicks.

Cracked Eggs

Sometimes one of the adults will chip an egg by mistake (usually with a claw), and if you notice such then gently seal the crack with something like nail polish or some-thing similar. Providing no germs have reached the embryo, then it has a good chance of hatching.

Chick Rearing

Throughout the breeding period—and for a short while before—the hen especially should have received a high-protein diet. Once the chicks have hatched, they will quickly put on weight. The adults should be given extra conditioners, such as brown bread and milk, which will be appreciated. If any chicks seem to be lagging behind their kin, then they can be removed and given supplementary feeds of something like a human baby food and to which a vitamin supple-ment has been added. It must be fed warm and be in a viscous state suitable to the age of the chick. Such extra feedings, say 2–4 over the day, can often help a chick catch up with its other nestmates. However, it should be stated that many species will not tolerate this sort of interference, which is better confined to peach-faced or masked, who are better established in captivity— the former rarely resent inspections. Once the chicks fledge, the cock will continue to feed them for maybe another ten days or so, and during this period you should watch things in the aviary very carefully. For example, a chick may have left the nest and as darkness approaches may still be on the aviary floor or clinging to the netting. In this position it could be attacked by cats, rats, night birds, or it could become chilled. Worse, it might rain, and this would do it no good at all because its feathers will not yet be waterproof enough to protect it. Such chicks should be placed back in the nest.

Another problem at fledging time is that the adults may start to attack the chicks. The hen especially may wish to get on with another round of eggs; cocks tend to attack their

sons. Once such attacks are noted, then remove the chicks straight away or you might find one or two badly injured or even dead. Peach-faced lovebirds have a bad reputation in this aspect, but they are by no means alone in the habit nor are they all as bad, and differing strains will react differently, which would

Closed rings can be carefully fitted on lovebird chicks by slipping it over the forward toes. The use of petroleum jelly often makes the job easier.

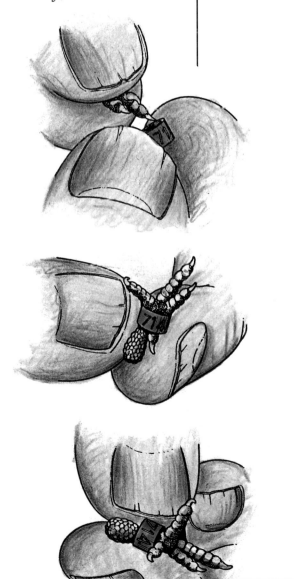

suggest that it is an inherited behavior.

Ringing

Not all breeders believe in ringing, or banding, as it is also called. The famed breeder of lovebirds (and other parrots) Jim Hayward in England is just one noted

From grotesque to cute; lovebird chicks at (top to bottom) three days; second down; and at 6 weeks. (Mervin F. Roberts and Michael Gilroy)

authority who dislikes ringing due to the risk of the birds getting caught up on such in netting, branches and such. Besides this risk are others. For example, should a bird damage its leg—the one which is closed rung—and if this swells, then unless the ring is removed very quickly by a vet the bird will probably lose that leg. Likewise, rung chicks must be checked regularly while in the nest to ensure that no feces or other debris has wedged between ring and

leg, as this will stop the blood flow

and a deformed leg at least may follow. I have seen a chick dragged out of the nest by a hen who had got a claw caught in the chick's ring, so each breeder must decide for himself whether the potential benefits of identification marking are worth the risk to the chicks. It must be stated that in the vast majority of cases there are no problems, but not in all cases.

Types of Ring You can purchase (state the species when ordering) closed metal and open metal rings as well as plastic rings in various colors. These latter rings can be used for temporary identification of chicks—but with lovebirds they rarely last long because the birds quickly destroy them. Closed rings are dated and numbered and placed on chicks a few days old. If the ring falls off, try it again a day or two later. It is slipped over the forward toes and up the shank. The rear toes are held in line with the shank, and with the aid of a sharp-ended matchstick you gently ease one, then the other, rear toe through the ring. A touch of petroleum jelly on the shank and rear toes will help. Rings can be ordered through clubs, pet shops or direct from suppliers advertising these in the avicultural press. For generations there has been a need to devise some non-risky form of identifying/marking of birds, and tattooing is the latest to receive attention. This is limited to larger birds though, so until a better method is found, then ringing remains the only workable option other than temporary means such as trimming certain feathers or staining feathers with a suitable color agent.

Fostering

Should the need arise, then eggs can be placed under the hens of other pairs—do not overburden a hen, however, if she already has a large clutch. Lovebird chicks have been reared by other parrot-like birds, but the problem is one of timing such that the foster birds have chicks of a similar size—this is crucial to the survival of the chicks. Again, if you are in a club, then another member may have suitable foster parents at that moment. If you seriously wish to become involved in hand-rearing a number of your lovebirds especially for the pet market, then I would advise you to purchase a book solely devoted to hand-rearing, as this is a subject all to itself and not possible to cover, with justice, in a work such as this.

A pair of lutino peach-faced lovebirds. Note that both of these birds have been ringed, probably as chicks. (Michael Gilroy)

Breeding Theory

A passel of fledgling peach-faced lovebirds. Note the odd lutino off to the side. (Michael Defreitas)

The dual objectives of any breeders of lovebirds are to both maintain quality of stock and, where color mutations are known, to produce birds of a preferred color. All features of lovebirds are controlled by genes, and these are found in all the bird's body cells as well as in the sex cells.

Genes are arranged along threadlike bodies known as chromosomes, which operate in pairs. Each gene along the chromosome has an equivalent gene on the opposite chromosome of a pair for the same feature, and features may be controlled by one or many pairs of genes. This means that there can be a considerable number of permutations of genes from one individual to another, and this accounts for the minor variations one can see in individual birds. In this chapter we shall look only at color, but all other features, internal or external, are controlled in the same manner—indeed the overall appearance of a bird (its phenotype) is the result of complex polygenic action. Some genes may express themselves when present in only a single dose; others need to be present in a double dose before they visually show themselves, while yet others may show themselves only partly if in single quantity—giving the illusion that the genes have blended. However, genes never mix like paint but always retain their own identity, regardless of whether or not they can be seen.

Mutations

In a normal, or wild type, lovebird the body color is mainly green, and this is because both of the genes which control the color are the same. However, every so often one of these genes may

expresses itself, and when this happens it is said to have mutated. Once a gene has mutated, then the trait follows one of the known patterns of inheritance. Genes are continually mutating, and it is by this means that speciation (and thus evolution) takes place. Most mutations in wild populations are not favorable to the individual carrying them, so the mutation is either lost or remains hidden for many years. A sudden change

A pair of young jade lovebirds. This strain's pale color would render it more conspicuous to predators in the wild. (Michael Gilroy)

of color can make a bird more noticeable to its predators or less acceptable to its own species. However, if such a mutated

suddenly change the way in which it

A fine specimen of the blue-masked lovebird, *Agapornis personata*. This is a mutation of the wild-type bird.

bird is captured, then the color can be selectively bred for, or the color may suddenly appear in aviary stock when chance brings together two birds, each carrying the mutant gene in single dosage. Exactly what causes a mutation to take place is not yet fully understood, though the effect is a change within the chemical make-up of the gene. The normal, or wild type, gene may have a number of mutant gene alternatives, and these are called *allelomorphs.* If the two genes for a given trait are the same, then the organism is termed *homozygous,* but if the gene on one chromosome differs in its expression from its counterpart gene then the organism is said to be *heterozygous.* Breeders should become familiar with these terms, and one or two others, as they will be

found to crop up continually in any text on the genetic aspects of breeding. As already stated, the visual form of a bird is known as its *phenotype,* while the genetic make-up of a bird is called its *genotype.* There are four patterns of gene inheritance that the breeder interested in hereditary should understand; this done, the keen enthusiast can then go on to to more detailed study through more specialized works devoted exclusively to genetics.

Autosomal Recessive Inheritance

An example of an autosomal recessive mutation is the blue form of the masked lovebird. In this type of mutation it does not matter which bird of a pair carries the mutant gene. It is termed *recessive* because if a bird carrying the mutation is paired to a normally colored bird, then the offspring will all appear as normal birds because the normal color is said to be dominant to this particular mutant gene. We can work out results of pairings involving recessive mutations by using letters to represent the individual genes. Where a gene is dominant, this is indicated

by giving it a capital letter, while the recessive is written in lower case. The mutated gene for blue will thus be *b* while the normal green color will be *B*. You will note that the same letter has been used to stand for green, and this is because in this case it is the alternative gene to the blue. Let us assume a purebreeding (homozygous) normal is paired to a purebreeding blue: these two birds will thus have the genotypes of *BB* and *bb*. Always remember that the genes are in pairs, one on each chromosome. The next thing to remember is that either of

the *B* genes can pair up with either of the *b* genes in the offspring resulting from the mating. In this case the only possible combination is *Bb*, which is a normally colored masked lovebird but one which carries the blue gene in its genotype. If we were to mate brother and sister from such offspring then the results would be as follows: *Bb* x *Bb* = *BB Bb bB bb* (*Bb* and *bB* are exactly the same). Thus we have 25% pure normals, 50% normal but carrying the blue gene, and 25%

The white-masked lovebird, another cultured mutation of *Agapornis personata*.

pure blue. There is no visual difference between the *BB* and *Bb* birds, and only a series of test matings will establish which are the purebreeding and which are the chromosome pair (double dose), while a dominant gene need only be present in a single dose to show itself. Another possible mating would be to pair a split bird with a pure recessive, and this would yield 50% normal/blue and 50% blues. This is the pairing we would use to test birds where

The pastel peach-faced lovebird. (Michael Gilroy)

heterozygous, or *split* birds. When birds are split for a color then this is written as normal/blue, the color in front of the line being visual while that behind it is hidden. From this mating it can be seen that before a recessive mutation can become visual it must be present on both of the genes of a we were not sure if they were pure normals or normals split for blue. Just one visual blue in a clutch would confirm that the normal was in fact a split bird, because otherwise we could not have obtained any visual blues. However, the fact that no blues appeared does not mean we can be sure that the bird was a purebreeding normal, and this is because theoretical expectations hold true over large numbers but not always in single or even two clutches.

The following colors have the same recessive mode of inheritance as that used in the example, and the results will be the same. (1) lutino in the red-faced, Nyasa, and in Fischer's lovebirds. (2) Blue in the peach-faced, masked, and Fischer's (also in the Nyasa it is believed, though the blues in both the last two species are thought to be the result of hybridization from the blue masked lovebird rather than distinct mutations in the species). (3) Golden cherry (American) in the peach-faced. (4) Golden cherry (Australian) in the peach-faced. (5) Golden cherry (Japanese) in the peach-faced.

Sex-linked Recessive Inheritance

The pair of chromosomes that determine sex are somewhat different from the other chromosome pairs (known as *autosomes*). In birds, the cock has two sex chromosomes of equal length, and these are designated as X chromosomes; the hen also has an X chromosome but the other of her pair is shorter and referred to as the Y chromosome. This latter chromosome does not have genes for color, and this affects the way in which colors are passed on to any offspring. A cock can be split for a sex-linked color but a hen cannot. We will see how this works using lutino as the example. Lutino is given the letter *i* in genetic calculations as this stands for *ino*, and this gene is responsible for producing both lutino and albino varieties. If we will pair a normal peach-faced cock to a lutino hen, the calculation will read: II x $iY = Ii\ IY\ Ii\ IY$. This translates as 50% normal/

Young jade lovebird. Note that this mutation retains some of the wild-type coloration on the throat and chest. (Michael Gilroy)

The American white, a color strain of the peach-faced lovebird. (H.R. Axelrod)

lutino cocks and 50% normal hens. The hens are to be regarded as purebreeding for their color, although they possess only one gene. Let us next pair one of the split-for-lutino offspring to a normal hen; this will yield 25% normal cocks, 25% normal hens, 25% normal/lutino cocks, and 25% lutino hens. Again the hens can be regarded as purebreeding for their color, and you will note that in them a sex-linked color expresses itself visually when only in single dose.

A third pairing could be a split-for-lutino cock to a lutino hen and this will produce 25% normal/lutino cocks, 25% normal hens, 25% lutino cocks, and 25% lutino hens.

The fourth pairing that can be done is that of a lutino cock to a normal hen, and this will produce 50% normal/lutino cocks and 50% lutino hens. You may notice the obvious ad-

vantage of such a mating because here we have no problems in sexing the young, as all the normal/lutinos must be cocks while any lutinos produced must be hens. Were we to pair the lutino cock to the lutino hens, then we would get 100% lutino cocks and hens. By having an understanding of genetic transmission it can be seen that one can calculate the genotype of a parent bird based on what colors turn up in a clutch. For example, if you did not know whether a given cock bird was homozygous or heterozygous for a sex-linked color, then pairing it to a sex-linked hen would be the way to find out about the cock, because if any mutations turned up then the cock must have been split for them. However, do remember the point about theory being based on large numbers, as this means that no mutations being produced does not absolutely show that the cock was a pure-breeding normal—it would take a few matings to be reasonably sure on this account.

The known sex-linked colors in lovebirds are: (1) lutino in peach-faced and (2) cinnamon in any lovebird species.

It can be mentioned that lovebirds are somewhat unusual in that most lutinos being bred are of the autosomal recessive type. Once sex-linked lutinos appear in species other than the peach-faced, then the non-sex-linked forms will probably become rare, if not lost to aviculture, because the sex-linked form is always much easier to produce. Both lutino and albino birds have poorer vision than do normal-colored birds, as the ino gene is linked to impaired eyesight.

Dominant Inheritance

In the two previous types of mutation the normal bird has genes which are always dominant to the mutated recessive genes, but there are a few muta-tions where the mutated gene is actually dominant to the wild color. In lovebirds the only dominant gene presently established is the pied. These birds can vary considerably from those which look quite normal other than for loss of pigment on the feet or of just a few feathers, to heavily variegated birds. The pied factor is extremely complex and it is not possible to tell in advance the degree of variegation that will result when pairing two pieds. The pied genes may be in single or double dose, these being referred to as single factor (s.f.) or double factor (d.f.). Whether a bird is single or double factor does not affect the bird's appearance, only the way it reproduces itself in the offspring. We will look at the various possible matings. However, firstly it should be stated that in the formulae used, a bird that is *Pp* is not a pied split for normal as might be thought based on previous calculations but it is a single-factor pied, the lower-case letter in this case standing for non-pied.

A pair of cinnamon lovebirds, a form of the lutino strain. (Michael Gilroy)

The jade lovebird. (Michael Gilroy)

A pied cannot be split for normal color, as the pied is a dominant gene; however, matters are made more complex because a recessive pied is known in lovebirds, though it is the so-called normal is in fact a pied but one in which the extent of the mutation is so slight that it cannot be seen; such birds will, however, be quite capable of producing well-marked pieds. Expectations are easily calculated as follows. A single-factor pied paired with a

thought to have died out. This means that birds sometimes sold as normals split for pied are most unlikely, and the truth is probably that normal (*Pp* x *PP* = *Pp Pp PP PP*) will yield 50% s.f. pieds and 50% normals. The pied factor can be transferred to other colors, so that when we talk of normals we could easily substitute blue for normal, so that one would get blue pieds. A s.f pied paired to a s.f. pied will produce 25% d.f. pieds, 50% s.f. pieds, and 25% normals. A d.f. pied paired to a s.f. pied will produce 50% d.f. pieds and 50% s.f. pieds. A d.f.pied paired to a normal will yield 100% s.f. pieds. Finally, if two d.f. pieds are paired, then all of the offspring will be d.f. pieds. It is important to remember that the factor for pied is independent of those responsible for the various colors, so calculations should always allow for this fact.

Incomplete Dominance

With the pied mutation, a bird either had the mutant gene, and it was visual, or it did not, in which case it exhibited the normal color—or its allelomorph. Only in terms of yield was it important whether the gene was in single or double quantity. However, in the case of partial, or incomplete, dominance, as is the case with the dark factor, the color of the bird will change depending on whether or not the gene is present in single or double dose, thus giving the illusion that the genes may have blended. Thus the depth of the color is modified from, say, a light green (normal) to a dark green (single factor, also called jade) to olive green (double factor). The same shades can be applied to blue, when they are termed dark blue (cobalt) or slate, respectively. Theoretical calculations are done in the same way as for the pieds, so only one example need be given. D indicates dark, while d means non-dark. If we pair a single factor bird with another, the expectations will be 25% double factor, 50% single factor, and 25% non-dark (Dd x Dd = DD Dd dD dd).

Other Considerations

When color mutations are bred, we can see the obvious changes that the mutation has made, but it is not possible to see what other effect the mutation may have had on the birds' internal metabolism. It

The jade color morph is the result of incomplete dominance of the mutant gene. (Michael Gilroy)

Blue and green pied lovebirds. The pied factor is complex and the outcome is difficult to predict in pairings of two pied lovebirds. (Michael Gilroy)

sometimes happens that along with the color mutation there has been another mutation that only shows itself over a period of time, or that has a degenerative effect on such qualities as breeding vigor, size or one of many other characteristics. For this reason it is essential that records be kept in order that one has a complete breeding history of one's stud as it develops. Such records will indicate the birds that have been paired, how many eggs were laid, how many were dead-in-shell, how many were reared without problem by their parents, and how good these turned out to be,

both visually and as breeding stock themselves. From such records it is possible to back-track should problems arise. It is never a sound policy to breed purely for the color of a bird at the expense of "type" (by which is meant the overall conformation of the bird), nor at the expense of traits such as good parental abilities, aggression and so on. The genetical aspect of breeding is a fascinating study in itself—but it is an area that breeders tend to love or loathe. Yet once the very basics are understood, it is surprising just how quickly one's interest in this develops; for this reason I would certainly recommend all lovebird breeders to take an interest in the subject. However, it is by no means an essential to being a successful breeder, as many top exhibition breeders have no genetical knowledge but compensate by having a good eye for a bird, and breeding is all about the combining of numerous aspects such as stock selection, good husbandry, good accommodation and a sensible attitude about how often pairs are allowed to breed or how often stock is exhibited.

Lovebirds as Pets

Lovebirds make super little pet birds, and while they are most unlikely to ever talk, they more than compensate with their lively and amusing characters. They are more robust than budgerigars and generally enjoy being on the move all of the time. They are not a species that should ever be kept as single birds—so do purchase a pair because these will be company for each other; single birds can be very sorry sights sitting all alone day after day, yet millions over the years have been subjected to such a terrible existence.

A lovebird may attain ten years or more in age, so will live as long as the average large dog. You will only get from a lovebird companionship in ratio to the efforts you put into its care and affection—the more you contribute, the more the lovebird will wish to respond to this. If you are not able to spend quite a bit of time with your birds then, frankly, you will not see them at their

best and might be better considering a tank of fish who will be quite happy as long as you feed them and keep their accommodation clean. Lovebirds are very social animals and are not an adornment to be fussed over initially and then left forgotten in the corner of the room when the initial excitement of owning them has worn off. It has already been stated that hand-reared lovebirds are by far the best purchase as pets, and it would be worth waiting for such a pair and paying out the extra these will cost—this is as nothing compared to the time and companionship they will give you in return. In actual fact, bearing in mind the tremendous extra work involved in hand-rearing birds, the prices charged for them are

Lovebirds appreciate the diversion of toys as much as any other parrot-like bird. (Michael Gilroy)

A blue masked lovebird on the wing. (Michael Gilroy)

ridiculously low at times.

An adult lovebird that has not already been tamed will require very considerable time spent with it, and will never compare with a hand-reared bird which has grown up with no fears of humans whatsoever.

Siting the Cage

It has been stated that an all-wire cage should be sited so as to give security along one side—two if possible. However, do not site this such that it is opposite a door, as drafts will almost certainly be created—and if there is one thing no bird can tolerate it is a draft, because in a cage it cannot escape this and so quickly chills. It is nice if your pets can be so positioned that they can see what is going on—they like to be involved with everything. Do not place the cage low down, as this creates stress in birds—the cage should be at about head height or just a piece lower, and it should be on a good firm base where it cannot be knocked over or rocked. If the cage can receive the early morning sunshine then this would be fine—and your pets will enjoy looking out of a window, where outside activities will keep their interest. But beware that strong sunlight—from which a bird cannot retreat at its convenience—is very damaging, so place some form of shade over part of the cage.

Cage Playthings

Lovebirds are quite playful and will enjoy various playthings. Some favorite lovebird toys include ladders, swings, bells, climbing chains, and mirrors. Keep in mind that your pet will be tempted to peck at anything within reach of his beak; therefore, all of his playthings should be durable and well made. Bird toys are modestly priced, and it is to your advantage—and your pet's—to buy only quality items.

Additionally, don't overcrowd your lovebird's cage with toys. It is better to offer him just one or two toys at a time. Some of the best playthings for a lovebird will be found to cost you nothing—or very little. For example, twigs of fruit trees will not only be good for your pets but will keep them amused for hours at a time—they are great whittlers. An old cotton bobbin is another handy little toy, and anything the lovebird can clamber up and down will be an amusement too. Do not clutter the cage with bits to the detriment of

flying space. A good idea is to provide a platform feeding station. These can be purchased or made to all manner of styles.

Basically, it consists of a platform which contains three or four feeding dishes around the edge, so they are not under any perches where they might be fouled. In the center of the platform you build a network of perches—rather like the climbing frames in parks used by toddlers. Your pets will look forward to leaving their cages and they will head straight for the platform, which can be on a table, shelf or freestanding on a pole. When they get tired, they will happily return to their cage for a sleep because in such a household the pet will regard its cage as a bedroom—not a prison, as can often be the case when birds are given no free-flying time.

Security
You must keep your eyes peeled for open doors,

A wide variety of safe and sturdy bird toys are available at well-stocked bird stores. (Michael Gilroy)

A fine example of the green pied lovebird. (Michael Gilroy)

windows, chimney openings and exhaust-fan outlets, all of which your pets might escape through. Fish tanks should have a canopy over them, so the birds are not at risk of drowning, and other pets, such as dogs or cats— especially the latter— should never be left unsupervised in a room with your lovebirds while these are out of their cage.

Loose electrical wires represent a danger to a lovebird, which might nibble on them and get a shock in more than one sense of the word! The kitchen is a very definite no-go area for your pets because it houses many hazards: stoves, open saucepans containing boiling water or hot food, food mixers, and maybe unguarded fans and other dangerous objects.

Molting

Birds normally molt once per year, and at such times they are likely to feel less than their cheerful selves, as it is a debilitating period. A molt can last about two or three months, and you can help your bird through this period by ensuring it receives twice a week a spraying with tepid water. In fact, it is advisable to spray your birds every week if they do not have access to their own bathing facilities, because it is through preening after bathing that the feather sheaths of new feathers are opened and allow good growth to follow. In the dry air of today's centrally heated homes it will often be found that birds may be in a slow, or "soft," molting condition throughout the year—this they seem to adjust to without undue problems.

Wing Clipping

Some owners will trim the flight feathers of their pets in order that they cannot escape too far should they get out of the house, or to prevent them flying around in the house. I do not think this is needed with lovebirds, who should be allowed to fly around the room, as this will keep them happy and in really fit condition. Should they escape the home, then, if the feathers are trimmed back too much, the birds cannot gain altitude and you have placed them at a big disadvantage because they will be unable to escape from dogs or cats.

If trimming is needed at all, let an experienced parrot handler attend to this for you. The feathers do not need a trimming that is unsightly; by cutting alternate feathers you can leave your pets with a limited flying power just while they become familiar to your home. At the next molt the feathers will regrow, by which time the birds can be allowed full flight in the home, which they will be well settled into.

Outdoors

When you go for a rest into your garden, then take your lovebirds, in their cage, with you. They will appreciate the change and the fresh air—indeed a light summer shower of rain will be beneficial to them; they will enjoy this Afterwards they should be returned to a warm room to dry. A really considerate family would provide an outdoor exercise aviary with branches in it so the pets have some time in which to enjoy nice spring or summer days.

Breeding

Pet lovebirds, assuming they are a true pair, have been known to breed in the confines of a cage, and if you wish to attempt this, then ensure their cage is large enough to contain a nest box. This should be kept moist, otherwise the eggs will suffer in too dry an atmosphere.

A pair of golden cherries on the bough. Cutting alternate flight feathers reduces the bird's power of flight yet leaves the wing's appearance intact, as in the bird on the left. (Michael Gilroy)

Health Matters

Lovebirds, like any other form of livestock, can suffer from a considerable number of ailments and diseases—so it is the object of the good stock person to reduce the incidence of risk to such by hygiene and to be aware of the situations most likely to encourage the spread of disease.

General Routine

Many problems can be avoided simply by applying strict routines to everyday situations. For example, do not move feeder pots from one aviary to the other—or water containers and so on. After washing, see that each utensil goes back into the same flight—you can easily mark the utensils with a number or other means of identification. Replace cracked dishes as soon as the crack or chip is seen; carry a number of spares. Replace perches at regular intervals. Always wash your hands after each bird you handle, and in the case of sick birds it is useful to keep a few pairs of disposable medical gloves, or at least thin rubber gloves, which can be sterilized after each bird has been handled. Cages and aviaries should be thoroughly washed down once a week and perches wiped with bleach rather than with household-brand

This masked lovebird displays all the signs of good health: clear eyes, good feathering, and a clean, sharply-edged bill. (Vince Serbin)

disinfectants, some of which may be too strong for the birds—your vet will recommend suitable solutions. With cages in particular, double check that corners are well cleaned and, after use, give all nesting boxes a very good cleaning, as these are prime places for lice and mites to hide in the crevices. Pet birds are at far less risk of illness than are aviary birds, but even

so the cage cleaning should be done with the same enthusiasm as is needed in a bird room.

The Sick Bird

Provided you are aware of your birds on an individual basis, then you will notice any that are not eating as normal or as sprightly as usual. These birds should be caught and placed into a hospital cage straight away, as the

sooner they are isolated the less risk of any illness being spread to other stock; a mild disorder promptly treated—such as a chill or diarrhea—will quickly be cured, but a mild disorder left for a day or two may progress into a

fatal problem. Never leave things overnight "to see how it looks tomorrow." The metabolic rate of birds is very fast compared to most other animals, which means illness proceeds at an equally fast pace, the more so in such small birds as lovebirds.

Quarantine

No additional stock should be added to your collection, regardless of how good its source of supply, until it has undergone 21 days of quarantine as far away from your main stock as is possible. During this time you can routinely treat the

Cage equipment and utensils should be checked for damage or wear and replaced when necessary. (Isabelle Francais)

birds for worms (unless this had already be done—do not forget to ask about this when purchasing). Worming via the drinking water is possible, though very unreliable, so have your vet or an experienced keeper show you how to de-worm by introducing the correct solution straight into the crop with plastic tubing and a syringe. This then can become a routine operation

The cremino peach-faced lovebird. (Eric Peake)

at least once a year in your aviaries. Pet birds are less likely to suffer from worms, as these are normally introduced via wild-bird droppings in the aviary, or via rodents' feces. If you do not opt to automatically de-worm your stock at set intervals, then make a routine collection of feces every so often and have these inspected microscopically by your

veterinarian, who will be able to make an egg count of worms and advise if worming is recommended at that time.

During quarantine you can also check that the birds have no mites, lice or other external parasites on them, and you may choose to treat them for these as a matter of course. Any of the proprietary anti-mite sprays or powders will kill the pests. They live by

sucking the blood of their host during the night and then hiding in crevices during the day (red mite), or they live out their whole life on the bird (lice) and spread by contact with other birds. In severe cases of infestation they will induce anemia and even death, especially in young chicks in the nest. They may cause the hen to abandon her chicks, and they may also introduce harmful bacteria into the tiny wounds they make for sucking blood. Once either has been identified, then you must burn all perches and subject the cage or nest box to a blow torch, this being the only sure way of killing unhatched eggs—merely treating the bird is not sufficient. Only when quarantined birds have been given a health check by yourself can they be introduced into the main collection. Show birds should also be subject to this period because they may have contracted an illness either at the show or possibly en route.

Wounds

Sooner or later you will have birds which get themselves bitten or caught up on something which creates a wound. Most such cuts will heal very quickly and will need no attention other than possibly being carefully wiped with a mild antiseptic or a styptic pencil. This applies even to lost toes, which often result from conflicts between

lovebirds in adjoining flights which were not double wired to prevent such contact. More serious wounds should receive veterinary treatment, in which case, clean the wound and then immobilize the bird by wrapping it in a cloth while you transport it to the surgery.

Injured Legs or Wings

A startled bird in a flight might dash itself against the wires or wall and as a result injure its legs or wing—maybe even breaking these. Veterinary help aside, there is not a lot you can do in such cases other than try to place the wing back into position, or place a match stick splint (but not too

An injured bird should be handled very carefully and placed in a quiet hospital cage for recovery. (Risa Teitler)

Wild-type masked lovebirds. These two bright-eyed individuals serve to illustrate the great popular appeal of lovebirds. (H. Reinhard)

tight) onto a broken leg. The injured bird should be placed into a hospital cage because you want to avoid chilling, given the bird's state of shock. Remove perches, and the wings or legs will usually right themselves—though they might thereafter be carried slightly out of position. Otherwise, they will be just fine.

Fits

Numerous parrots occasionally suffer from fits of one sort or another. They will twist their heads about in an uncontrolled manner or will slump to the cage floor twitching and then go very still. Place them in a warm spot, out of bright lights, to recover—there is little else you can do for them at the time. The causes may be hereditary, built-up stress, or the result of a nutritional deficiency. Your vet will treat with a suitable supplement and maybe an antibiotic.

Swellings

A swelling may simply be the localized reaction to an external intrusion into the skin (such as a wasp sting or similar), in which case it need only be carefully, and daily, swabbed with a suitable antiseptic until it recedes or bursts. However, swellings in birds are usually the results of other complaints, such as tumors, and in either case should be referred to your vet for treatment.

Respiratory Problems

If you notice a bird is gasping for breath or wheezing when breathing—with maybe a discharge from its nose—then it is suffering from some form of respiratory disorder, and so should be isolated and subjected to hospital-cage heat treatment. Once this is in hand, do not then transport it to the vet because the drop in temperature will do more harm than good—lovebirds make very poor surgery patients anyway. Have your vet do a house call for treatment—it will cost more but the chances of success will increase.

Diarrhea

The problem with diarrhea is that it is a symptom of just about every major illness you could think of! A mild form may be just the result of a chill or eating too much greenfood after having received little of this. If it persists after hospital-cage treatment for 24 hours

(during which time only seed and water should be offered), then lose no time in consulting your vet—and have available samples of the feces which may be required for microscopy.

Clinical Signs

It may be noticed that no antibiotics, medicines or such have been cited in this text. The reason for this is that it is not difficult to list one remedy after the other—nor is it difficult to

A bird that spends much of its time in this position should be checked for illness! (F.W. Huchzermeyer)

Pastel blue (left) and cobalt strains of the peach-faced lovebird. (Michael Gilroy)

catalog diseases, but beyond filling up text these have little meaning to the average bird keeper—and may even be dangerous if they result in attempts at home treatment of problems that only a qualified veterinarian could hope to treat. Most avian diseases have the same clinical signs: diarrhea, weeping eyes, discharging nostrils, loss of appetite, fluffed up feathers, possibly vomiting, and usually loss of weight. The cause can be respiratory, it could be the result of a disease of the alimentary system, the liver or kidneys, spleen, or it could be a viral infection—or it could be a number of complaints, one inducing the other. Home treatment is fine if you are an expert on gram-positive and negative bacteria and if you are totally informed on the reaction to these of the many antibiotics now available. If you

are not, then the wrong choice could be fatal to your birds, and as most diseases are only confirmed by microscopy it is always better to leave bird treatments to veterinarians. In years gone by the price of birds was lower than the likely vet's bill, and this meant birds either recovered from illness without treatment, were helped by home remedies, or they died. Generally, vets had little experience with birds as a direct result. Today, things have changed dramatically, for the high cost of most birds is such that professional treatment is worthwhile, and most vets now have good experience with birds—as well as with other pets, such as snakes, which were formally regarded as very exotic. Research is being conducted in avicultural species, so it will be cheaper in the long run to establish a good relationship with a local veterinarian who is now much informed on latest treatments. The best a breeder can do is to totally concentrate on the good-husbandry side, for this will do much to prevent illness. Should a bird die without exhibiting any clinical

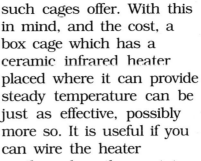

such cages offer. With this in mind, and the cost, a box cage which has a ceramic infrared heater placed where it can provide steady temperature can be just as effective, possibly more so. It is useful if you can wire the heater through a thermostat so that a constant temperature is assured. The heater can be placed at one end of the cage, outside, and this will provide the correct local temperature, which will be slightly less at the other end of the cage. If the bird is not happy directly in line with the heater, it can move to a somewhat cooler, though still warm, spot. The fact that the breeder cage has bars, rather than glass, ensures it will be well ventilated, which is important in such a cage. Only seed and water should be placed into such. The extra heat may well do wonders on its own, but its side effect is to create thirst. Prescribed treatments may be water soluble, and so may be given via the water in mild cases of infection. The temperature range in a hospital cage should be about 30–34°C (86–93°F) to be effective. Once the bird shows improvement, then

Adhering to the basic principles of good husbandry will go a long way in keeping your lovebird healthy. (Michael Gilroy)

signs of illness, then it is recommended that it be sent for a post-mortem to establish cause of death. The cost is small, and numerous laboratories now advertise such a service— your vet may even do such as well. This can save you a lot of worrying and it might pin-point a problem you may be able to overcome once you know the cause.

Hospital Cages

There are numerous commercially made units available, often glass fronted, but beyond being rather expensive they are not always the best to obtain for parrot-like birds. Once a bird is totally sealed into such cages, that is by virtue of the glass, they tend to become greatly stressed, and this undoes much of the benefit

it must be acclimatized back to the normal housing temperature by reducing the hospital-cage temperature a few degrees each day until it is back at normal. Breeders are strongly urged to acquire a hospital cage, which is worth its weight in gold. The progressing developments in both infrared heaters and in ultraviolet and other specialized lamps, I feel sure, will result in even more superior hospital-cages in the future.

Overgrown Beaks and Claws

Both beaks and claws may sometimes become overgrown due to incorrect perch size or insufficient hard materials for the birds to keep their beaks in trim. These are easily clipped back to a correct size. With the claws, trim so that you do not cut into the blood supply, which can easily be seen in light-colored claws. In those which are darker, a beam from a flash light should show the supply up, but otherwise just take less off. The beak is trimmed in the same manner and with the same care in respect of blood vessels. Your vet will attend to this if you are unsure or do not have suitable clippers—sharp scissors will deal with the claws but guillotine nail clippers used for dogs are better for beaks—or use standard nail trimmers of a suitable size.

Feather Plucking

Should your birds start to pluck their feathers, then this often signifies boredom but may also have a nutritional or hereditary basis. Firstly, supply plenty of twigs for the bird to amuse itself with. If it is happening to a bird kept indoors all of the time, then a spell in an aviary may distract its attention from plucking and the extra exercise may bring about a cure. Carefully detail everything you feed to your pets and have your vet look over this to see if there is a problem or omission. If the cause is actually another bird doing the plucking, then remove the culprit. Of course, birds may pluck their feathers during the breeding season to help line their nests, so do not confuse this with habitual plucking.

The Lovebird Species

The nine species of lovebirds are contained in the genus *Agapornis* and there are in all some 15 subspecies. All are of African distribution, with the Madagascar being found on the offshore island of that name, as well as on nearby islands where it has been introduced by man. One species, *Agapornis swinderniana*, is unknown to aviculture and familiar only from skins in various museum collections. The most widely distributed species is the red-faced, *A. pullaria*, while the smallest distribution is seen in the black-cheeked lovebird, *A. nigrigenis*. In size, lovebirds range from the Abyssinian, *A. taranta*, the largest, through to the Nyasa, *A. lilianae*, which is the smallest. Before briefly giving details of each species and their color mutations, it is useful for would-be enthusiasts to have a basic understanding of how birds are classified, as such a grounding will be found of benefit when reading other texts and avicultural papers.

The red-faced lovebird. *Agapornis pullaria*. (A.J. Mobbs)

Classification

The object of what is termed the binomial system of classification is to group animals in a convenient manner such that they can be referred to on a collective basis without the need to name individuals—information upon all members within a given group being common to its members at that rank or taxon. At the apex of this triangle is the kingdom Animalia, while along the base line are all the individual species and their subspecies, together with their variations. Between these levels are numerous ranks, which are arrang ed such that their members are related—be this supposedly or real. Any rank above the level of a species must, of necessity, be man-made, or artificial, though the system itself is considered to be as near to a natural system as can be devised.

At each level an archetypal example was chosen and all other animals are compared to this based an a number of similarities. Rarely does any animal have a single diagnostic feature, so animals are grouped based on numerous features. The aviculturist is interested in the rank called a class and all ranks below this. Birds are in the class Aves, and this is divided into 27 orders, examples being Falconiformes (hawks, eagles, falcons), Strigiformes (owls), Anseriformes (ducks, geese and swans), and so on. Lovebirds are contained in the order Psittaciformes: the parrots and parrotlike birds.

Upper: *Agapornis lilianae*, the Nyasa lovebird; Lower: *A. nigrigenis*, the black-cheeked lovebird.

The parrots, based on numerous features, are divided into three families: Loriidae small birds, typically short-tailed, possessing relatively large beaks for their size, and mainly green in color but with differing head colors in particular. Based on these differences, the genus is divided into a number of groups, which are similar in all but the smallest of details, and these groups are the species, each of which forms a naturally free-breeding population. However, even within such a similar group of birds there may be some members that consistently show small variations, (the lories and lorikeets), Cacatuidae (the cockatoos), and Psittacidae (the true parrots).

There are obviously many different sorts of parrots, so Psittacidae is divided into many genera, such as *Amazona* (amazon parrots), *Aratinga* (conures) and *Loriculus* (hanging parrots), and others in which the members of the genus are by now looking very similar to each other and clearly different from other birds which are nonetheless quite clearly parrots. Lovebirds are all contained in the genus *Agapornis*, and all are

Left: museum specimen of *A. swinderniana*, the black-collared lovebird. Below: an artist's rendering of the species, which is rarely seen in captivity. (Eric Peake)

An adult male gray-headed lovebird, *Agapornis cana*. The female is similar but lacks the extensive gray area, it being replaced by a pale green. (San Diego Zoo)

so these are identified as sub-species to the main breeding populations, and it is at subspecific level that we can see evolution in progress. Beyond the ranks cited, there are numerous other ranks between these but those cited are the most important to remember.

The Species

The nine lovebird species can be divided into two distinct groups with two species being intermediate between these.

Dimorphic Species

Agapornis cana cana (Gmelin, 1788) — Madagascar lovebird

Size 13cm (5in)

Color The cock has its upperparts of head, neck, nape and upper chest of very light gray; the wings and back are dark green while the

On the one side there are the sexually dimorphic species; on the other there is the white-eye-ring group, while the peach-faced lovebirds are considered to be intermediary between these groups. It is thought that those of the white-eye-ring group are phylogenetically older.

underparts are a light yellow-green. The beak is a whitish gray, as are the feet. The irides are brown. Hen as for the cock, but the gray parts of the head and chest are replaced by light green to the front, getting darker as they progress to the nape of the neck and head.

In Aviculture This species was first imported into

Europe during the latter part of the 19th century and has had a somewhat checkered history. Its price has fluctuated quite widely with the imposition of import bans at various times. However, during the years when stock was freely available, little real efforts were placed into establishing domestic strains, with the result that today there are none of the species in Australia, while in the UK and USA breeding is sporadic. The overall breeding record is very poor when the numbers imported over the years are considered. They do little nest building, so are happy with a somewhat smaller nest box than other lovebirds. A problem with them is that they are not free-breeding year 'round and prefer to nest in the autumn, which is where part of the breeding problem with them lies. They cannot be considered hardy birds and appear susceptible to lung disease—a dichloros strip as used in many insecticides should be hung near their cage during the winter and this will remove the problem. They are rather nervous birds prone to death by fright, so should be given aviaries screened by shrubs for added security. They will breed in roomy indoor flights and cages, so while they may not be the easiest species to establish it is likely that efforts to do so would be worthwhile, given the fact that exports from their homeland will probably remain patchy to nonexistent. Soaked seed, a vitamin supplement and possibly rice are appreciated by them. The beginner would be advised to gain experience with easier species with a view to then trying this pretty lovebird.

Subspecies: A. c. ablectanea Bangs 1918. Darker green coloration with less yellow and a more grayish head.

Agapornis pullaria pullaria (Linnaeus,1758) — red-faced lovebird
   Size 15cm (6in)
   Color The male

Green (left) and blue pied lovebirds. (Michael Gilroy)

The black-winged lovebird, *Agapornis taranta*.

is an all-green bird with a bright orange-red face. The red extends from the mid-crown down the side of the head, creating a line about mid-eye level and continuing to the upper throat. The beak is red and the feet gray. The feathers of the back and wings are darker than those of the under-parts. The female is similar, but the red is more orange and does not create such a straight line of demarcation with the green, but merges into this with almost yellowish feathers; the beak is pale red to horn colored.

In Aviculture Although this is the oldest known species, first imported into Europe during the 16th century, it has proved the most difficult to breed. This is due to the fact that in the wild it builds its nest directly in a termite's nest, often found high in the trees, occasionally at ground level. The female digs out a tunnel before excavating a large orange-sized chamber. The male attempts to help but appears to be less than efficient. The termites, normally aggressive, do not bother the lovebirds, and seal up any of their own tunnels that lead to the lovebird nest. Individual breeders in the UK, Germany, Switzerland and Portugal have had the most success with the species, which is unusual in being a colony breeder. The species also has the sweetest voice of any lovebird. However, it is also the most nervous species and must be acclimatized with considerable care lest it falls down dead from quite simple operations, such as being caught up or even from a slamming door!

It must be able to burrow in order to build a nest, so peat or cork have been shown to be the best materials—packed into a box or a small container. The latter material reduces the risk of the ceiling caving in on the chicks, which can happen when peat is used. It has also been found that heating of the nest chamber once the eggs have hatched is important. Heater pads giving a constant temperature of about 27°C (81°F) will neatly

reduce the risk of the chicks becoming chilled when the parents leave the nest. Humidity is retained by the hen bathing, thus having wet plumage when she returns to sit with the chicks. The youngsters consume large quantities of mealworms, so an insectile food as supplied to softbills should be supplied along with a wide range of fruits, including figs. Once the youngsters fledge, the next problem is keeping them warm when they leave the nest, so in the

The red-faced lovebird, *Agapornis pullaria*. The sexes in this species are very similar, except that the red in the female is paler and not as sharply delineated from the green as in the male.

Agapornis taranta (Stanley, 1814) — Abyssinian, or black-winged, lovebird

Size 16.5cm (6in)

Color The male is an all-green bird with a red forehead, lores and red feathered eye rings. The flight feathers and underwing coverts are black, and the tail feathers carry black barring. The irides are brown and the feet are gray: beak is pale red. The female is similar but has no red at all other than her beak.

In Aviculture Although this is an extremely hardy species, it has failed to become a well-established breeder in captivity in comparison with the top three lovebirds. It can be wintered outdoors as it has to contend with sub-zero temperatures in its homeland overnight—though daytime temperatures are quite warm. It will use a smallish nest box in order to keep snug and warm at night. Formerly bred in Australia, it is believed that stocks

Lovebirds are strong, swift fliers, and full-flighted birds will be a challenge to catch if they effect an escape from their quarters! (R. & V. Moat)

cooler regions the aviary flight should be enclosed with plastic panels, except for one small area. Again, this is not a species for the beginner; but for the more advanced lovebird keeper, having available space, the species should afford an interesting challenge, and once a well-established strain was built-up, where the birds were less nervous, then the high price the species commands should repay the higher costs that would be needed for success.

Mutations Both pied and recessive lutino mutations have been bred.

Subspecies: A. n. ugandae Neumann 1908, also *A. p. guineensis.*

have now died out. It is bred throughout Europe, the UK and the USA but only on a small scale. Sexing youngsters cannot be done with certainty until after the first full adult molt at about 8–9 months of age. No color mutations are available, though Rosemary Low reports a cinnamon in 1977, but this did not become established.

Subspecies Some authors give *A. t. nana* Neumann 1931 but others do not accept this as valid, as it shows only extremely minor difference in the size of beak and wings, which may be no more than variants which would be normal in any population.

Intermediate Species

Agapornis swinderniana swinderniana (Kuhl, 1820) — Swindern's, or black-collared, lovebird

Size 13.5cm (5in)

Color The most striking feature of this species is the fact that it has a black beak. It is otherwise an all-green lovebird, the color being lighter on the underparts and darkest on the wings, which have small amounts of red and blue on their tips. The feet are gray and the irides yellow. A black band encircles the rear half of the neck.

Artist's rendering of the black-winged lovebird, *A. taranta*. Sexual dimorphism is more marked in this species than in most other lovebird species in that the female shows no red other than on the bill. (Eric Peake)

Below the band the feathers are yellow or brownish, depending on the subspecies. These colors extend completely round the neck and onto the upper chest.

In Aviculture All attempts to keep these birds alive, let alone breed, have failed. Only very rarely have they been imported into Europe or the USA. In the Congo a Father Hutsebout from Sweden was able to keep them alive only if figs were continually available. Given the length of time they have been known, it is a remarkable fact that they have proved so elusive to observe and maintain in captivity—a real challenge to aviculture when someone is able to acquire a number of pairs.

Subspecies: A. s. zenkeri Reichenow 1895; *A. s. emini* Neumann 1908.

Agapornis roseicollis roseicollis (Vieillot, 1817) — peach-faced lovebird

Size 15cm (6in)

Color Both sexes are similar. The overall color is green, which is typically lovebird in that it is darker on the wings and lighter on the under-parts. The face is a soft pinkish red, which extends down to the upper chest, round the sides of the face and upwards behind the eyes and then across the crown. The beak is horn colored, the irides are dark brown and the feet are gray. There are blue feathers on the rump, and there is barring of black on the tail feathers.

A pair of adult black-winged lovebirds. The male is on the left. Art by R.A. Vowles.

In Aviculture Although originally discovered in 1793, the species was not named until 1817 because it was thought to be a subspecies of the red-faced, a somewhat surprising conclusion given the obvious differences between them. The species was first bred in Europe during 1869, and they immediately became very popular birds. However, two world wars depleted stocks and resulted in much hybridization with other species, while the 1930 parrot ban in the UK did nothing to help during the inter-war years. However, the peach-faced, along with the masked and Fischer's, managed to retain a nucleus of breeders when the other species steadily lost enthusiasts—or these changed over to the more reliable breeding habits of the popular three.

Today it is probable that the peach-faced is bred by more people than all of the other species put together, and the many color mutations have obviously influenced the increasing number of breeders to this species. It is a popular show bird and can be well recommended to beginners. Because they are very prolific, it is better to restrict each pair to no more than three rounds per year (two would be better), and breeding should not be encouraged between birds that are too young; a good age would be after 9 months old, by which time the birds will be mature and in full adult plumage.

The black-collared lovebird. (Eric Peake)

Opposite, top to bottom: American pied light green peach-faced; masked; yellow masked; Dutch blue Ino peach-faced. Photo courtesy Vogelpark Walsrode.

Though hens are invariably dominant to cocks in all lovebird species, this is not always so, and numerous breeders report cocks which dominate their hens in this species.

There are many breeders of peach-faced in Australia, where the species and color mutations are well established. These birds will happily accept any form of nest box and rarely resent inspection. They are not to be trusted with other species or even their own kind—while maybe not as vicious as those from the wild of a few years ago, this is a relative term and they can still be very aggressive, even toward their own youngsters once these fledge.

Mutations There are more color mutations in the peach-faced than in any other lovebird. The yellow is an especially attractive color, this replacing all of the green areas and contrasting nicely with the orange-red face. The pieds vary considerably, as is normal with this mutation, while the white-faced blues will appeal to those liking this color. Another mutation is the pastel

blue—it is actually a dilute green rather than a blue, and here the red of the face is changed to ivory gray on the throat and a pinkish color to the forehead. One of the latest mutations is the so-called cinnamon, which looks more like a dilute version of the normal color rather than what you might expect something called cinnamon to look like. There is no doubt that in the coming years further mutations will appear in the species and, with recombinations of existing colors, there may yet come a time when the peach-faced all but rivals the budgerigar in the number of colors that are available; and given the fact that it has red, which the budgerigar does not, it may even surpass it.

Subspecies: A. r. catumbella Hall 1955. This has a lighter color overall than the nominate race but the forehead red is darker and the cheeks more orange.

White-Eye-Ring Species
Agapornis fischeri Reichenow 1887 — Fischer's lovebird
   Size 14cm (5in)

Color Both sexes are similar. The general body color is green, dark above and lighter below. The forehead and upper throat are bright orange, this giving way to a yellow about the area of the upper chest, and the yellow forms a variable collar extending round to the lower nape of the neck. The cheeks are orange, which gradually changes to olive yellow as it moves around the neck. The beak is orange-red with a gray cere, and there is a white border around the eyes. Irides are brown and the legs are gray. The rump is blue, and blue also tips the tail feathers.

In Aviculture This species has proved extremely adaptable, and various introductions of aviary stocks, either deliberately as at the port of Tanga (Tanzania) or via escapees, proved a success and colonies established themselves. Fischer's are hardy, somewhat noisy, but invariably good breeders. They will readily hybridize, but this is not to be encouraged. The species is established in Australia but somewhat scarce, so higher priced.

Mutations There are a few mutations in the Fischer's, one of which is the yellow. This is not a true lutino but a dilution of the normal green; it is rather mottled, somewhat like a pied, and the tips of the flight feathers are gray white. A true lutino was recorded in France but appears to have been lost. There are blue forms of the Fischer's in the UK, and hybridization with blue masked lovebirds has also resulted in blues. It is likely we shall see considerable progress in the color breeding of this species over the coming years.

Subspecies None have been recorded.

Agapornis personata (Reichenow, 1887) — masked lovebird

Size 14cm (5.5in)

Color The sexes are similar. As is normal in the genus the body color is green, darker on the upperparts and lighter on the undersides. The head is covered by a hood of black which gives way to a yellow collar around the neck and which extends well down the chest to the abdomen. The beak is orange-red, and there is the white eye-ring of bare flesh, as well as a gray-white cere. The irides are brown and the legs gray.

In Aviculture This species first arrived in Europe

A lovely pair of adult Fischer's lovebirds. (Michael Gilroy)

during 1925 and quickly became popular—as it did in the USA and Australia. It is a hardy species, and many Australian breeders propagate it on a colony system. Masked lovebirds will use most nesting materials, and these are often dipped into the water dish, assumedly to both soften them and to help retain humidity in the nest. They will breed throughout the year if allowed to, but summer clutches are always to be recommended if possible.

Mutations The blue masked lovebird was the first mutation to become available and came from wild stock. It was sold to the London Zoo in 1927 and formed the basis of numerous strains in Europe. However, these failed to really become established. The situation in the US was totally different, and in California success was considerable. Francis Rudkin Sr. was especially successful with this mutation and was probably responsible for its spread in the USA. After the Second World War, American imports greatly helped the British enthusiasts to really

Top to bottom: black-cheeked; gray-headed; yellow-masked; red-faced. Photo courtesy Vogelpark.

establish the color in the UK. Large numbers were also imported from Japan, where it had become cheaper than the normal wild type. However, the Japanese strains did not prove as suited to the UK as did those from the USA, which were very good both in size and breeding vigor. In this color the green area become blue, while the yellow feathers become white—the black mask remains unchanged but the beak becomes a pale pink. A yellow mutation appeared about 1935 in the USA, but this is a dilution mutation rather than a lutino. A somewhat more yellow masked has been produced in Denmark and in that same country has appeared a white masked lovebird (without mask) and an orange-breasted masked lovebird. However, in neither of these latter two cases have any similar offspring been produced, so it is probable the colors were brought about by metabolic disorders that affected the chemical make-up of the pigments, instead of a gene mutation. Amongst other colors now being bred are albinos, lutinos, cinnamons, pieds and pastel blue (dilute green), but all are still in the very early stages of development.

Subspecies None have been recorded.

Agapornis lilianae Shelley 1894 — Nyasa lovebird
Size 13cm (5in)
Color Sexes are similar, and the color is very like that detailed for the Fischer's lovebird but the orange-red areas are marginally less intense in color. The rump is green as opposed to blue in the Fischer's.

In Aviculture This species was, for thirty years, considered to be a form of the peach-faced lovebird, a rather amazing conclusion to make given the obvious differences—the eye-ring for one. It was named for Lilian Sclater by Shelley. The first Nyasas to reach Europe arrived in 1926, and in fact bred within months of this. They proved extremely prolific here, as they did in the USA and Australia. However, in each of these countries stock has degenerated over the years and for some unknown reason they continue to decline in numbers, so that they are now becoming very expensive. In Australia for many years, though less so today, all lovebirds were called Nyasas, which led to obvious confusion within the genus. They can be colony bred and, along with the red-faced, are probably the least aggressive of the lovebird species. They build domed nests but will happily accept whatever alternative is supplied to them.

Mutations The only mutation that is established is the lutino, an impressive bird of yellow, with white flight feathers and the head making a good contrast, being red. However, as with the normals, this mutation is less seen than in past years. Because it is an autosomal recessive it is more difficult to perpetuate than were it sex-linked, which most lutino mutations generally are.

Subspecies None have been recorded.

Agapornis nigrigenis W. L. Sclater, 1906 — black cheeked lovebird

Size 14cm (5.5in)

Color Sexes similar. Body color green, darker above than below. The forehead is a chocolate (dark) brown becoming black on the cheeks. The upper breast is orange, as is the nape of the neck. The

Peach-faced lovebird. (R.V. Moat)

beak is orange-red, the eye-ring white and the irides brown. The feet are gray.

In Aviculture It is quite surprising that given the prolific manner with which this species reproduces its own kind that it has become a rarity in aviaries. It was the last species of lovebird to be identified yet quickly established itself in the early part of the 20th century. However, large numbers of imports resulted in a loss of breeding interest, which has been unfortunate, as the present poor breeding state illustrates. It is believed to have died out in Australia, where it was hybridized with other species. It is to be hoped that more people will take up the species because, given its very small range of distribution, any major disturbance to its habitat would mean it would be very vulnerable to dramatic reduction in its wild population.

Mutations A blue mutation is reported from Denmark but as yet is not well established.

Subspecies None are reported or likely within such a confined distributional area.

Cinnamon lutino lovebird. (Michael Gilroy)